Professional
Secrets of
WEDDING PHOTOGRAPHY

Douglas Allen Box

AMHERST MEDIA, INC. ■ BUFFALO, NY

DEDICATION

A special thanks to all the brides and grooms, along with their families, for trusting me to tell the story of their wedding. By allowing me to photograph their special day, they allowed me to become a part of their family for a day. I had the responsibility of recording the emotions and personality of the day. To do that, you have to get to know the people. You have to see into their souls.

Copyright ©2000 by Douglas Box.
All photographs by Douglas Box.
All rights reserved.

Published by:
Amherst Media, Inc.
P.O. Box 586
Buffalo, N.Y. 14226
Fax: 716-874-4508

Publisher: Craig Alesse
Senior Editor/Project Manager: Michelle Perkins
Assistant Editor: Matthew A. Kreib
Scanning Technician: John Gryta

ISBN: 0-936262-92-3
Library of Congress Card Catalog Number: 98-74594

Printed in the United States of America.
10 9 8 7 6 5 4 3 2 1

TABLE OF CONTENTS

While visiting with a prospective client on the phone one day, I asked the bride, "Are photographs important to you?" Her answer changed the way I thought about weddings. She replied, "Of course, that's why we are having a wedding!"

Chuckling, I commented, "I thought that was what the groom is for." Insightfully, she continued, "The groom is for the marriage, the reason for the wedding is to share it with friends and family and to record it for posterity!"

She was right. The marriage is about the love the bride and groom share with each other. You can have a marriage without planning a special wedding event. The wedding is an event designed to allow the couple to share this special day with the people they care about the most.

This means that our job as wedding photographers is multifaceted. We must:

> "The wedding is about sharing this special day with the ones the couple cares about most."

- *Capture the emotion.* Show the personality of the wedding, the way the bride dreamed it would be.
- *Record the details.* Preserve the little things that make her wedding different from every other wedding in the world.
- *Show her beauty.* This is one of the most important days in her life and she will never look more radiant. Our job is to put her on film in all her beauty.
- *Give her peace of mind.* Once she hires you, the bride and her family don't want to have to worry about photography. She trusts you. She trusts that you will create beautiful images and be professional.

In this book, you will learn the skills you need to accomplish all of these objectives, from taking top-notch wedding portraits, with beautiful lighting and elegant posing, to working with your clients and their guests to make being photographed by you a good experience for everyone involved.

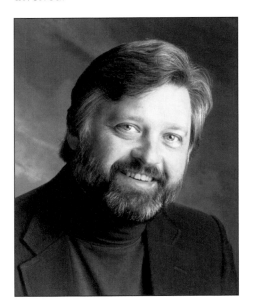

ABOUT THE AUTHOR:
Doug Box is a professional photographer who has been photographing weddings since 1972 and has since photographed hundreds of couples' nuptials. Doug is also a successful portrait photographer and studio owner who lectures frequently on wedding and portrait photography. He is the author of *Professional Secrets for Photographing Children*, available from Amherst Media, Inc.

OUTDOOR PHOTOGRAPHY

There is something special about natural light. It is somehow more expressive.
Light can evoke emotion. Light is the lyrics of photographs.
Capturing the beauty of outdoor light can produce truly memorable images.

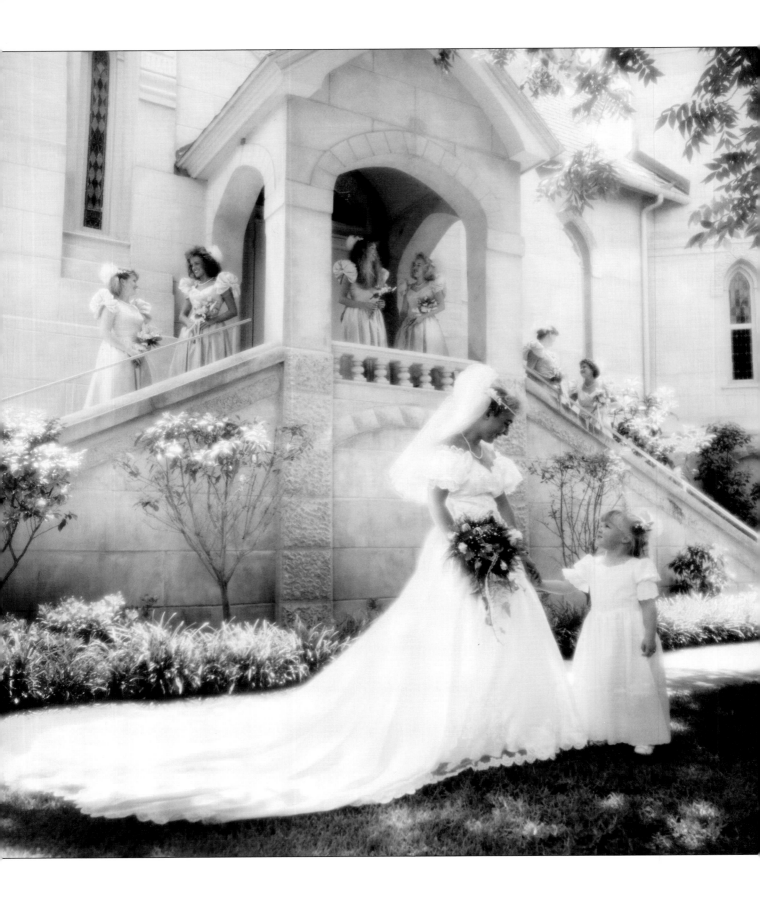

"The bride and the flower girl seem to have a more important role in the photograph."

☐ Pose

I asked the girls to space themselves on the steps. I brought the bride and flower girl to the foreground and just let them be themselves. The image has a very spontaneous look. It also has a beautiful design for the story of the wedding. The posing gives the image much more interest than a simple line of bridesmaids. The bride and the flower girl seem to have a more important role in the photograph, reflecting their important roles in the wedding.

☐ Props and Background

The background (the front of the church) is the prop. You go up the stairs to the sanctuary. The stairs provide great separation for the girls, giving each her own space and placing emphasis on the foreground. I feel it is important to show the environment of the day – after all, the bride chose this church for a reason.

☐ Photography

I used the 80mm lens on the Hasselblad for this portrait. The image was made when the sun was high in the sky, although I wish it would have been later in the day. I don't particularly like the bright strip of sunlight behind the bride. A cloudy day, or shooting later in the day, would have helped eliminate this. But, as a wedding photographer, you need to make the best image possible, no matter what the situation. To minimize the width of the light area, I lowered the camera and put the bride and flower girl in the shady area in the foreground. I did not use the flash because it would have made the foreground subjects too bright compared to the background. I wanted them to stand out against the light grey stone.

☐ Psychology

When working with children, I usually talk softly and playfully. The first rule of wedding photography is to remember that, even though you have a job to do, you also have to be pleasant and polite. This is their special day; don't ruin it by being pushy.

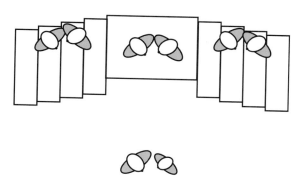

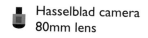

Hasselblad camera
80mm lens

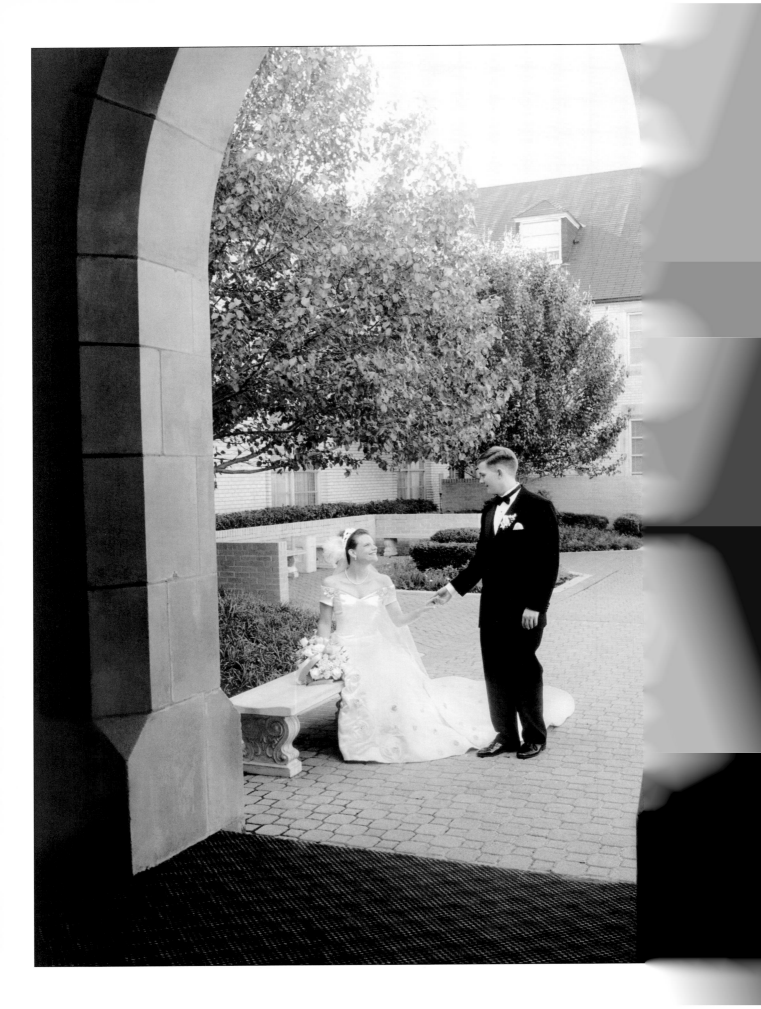

"It gives you the feeling you've just walked up on this scene..."

□ **Pose**

What could be more natural and sweet than the groom extending his hand to help up the bride? They're all alone, having a private moment. I was there to capture it, and to capture their love for each other.

□ **Prop**

I used the arch as a significant part of the image. It gives you the feeling you've just walked up on this scene and separates the viewer from the subjects. This gives them a sense of privacy. The arch also adds depth to the image. Use your hands to cover the arch and you'll see that it changes the whole image.

□ **Background**

This is the courtyard just outside of the church where the ceremony took place. The bench is a natural part of the scene. If you ask a bride to sit on something like this that might be rough or not perfectly clean, be sure to lift the dress and have the bride sit on the petticoat. Then carefully place the gown down behind her to avoid getting it scuffed or dirty.

□ **Photography**

I used the 50mm lens on the Hasselblad to give the perspective needed to include the arch. To meter, I used the Sekonic L508 in the incident mode and the flat disk setting. The best way to meter a situation like this is to walk up to the subjects and read the meter "at" the subject. However, on occasions when you're trying not to spoil the mood, you can meter at a place that has the same light as on the subject. For this image, I stepped out from under the porch to the right and metered the light there. Because the light was soft, late afternoon light and about the same value in the whole area, I was able to make a fairly accurate reading without disturbing the couple.

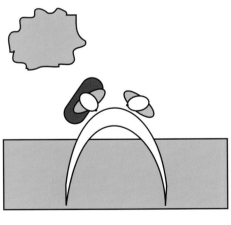

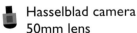 Hasselblad camera
50mm lens

□ Pose

There is no posing here. For images like this, just record the story, and don't be stingy with the film. Take plenty of exposures. Many times you will end up with a great series like this.

□ Background

This series, as the name implies, documents the arrival of the groom at the bride's home, where we began the photography. The props are the natural accessories of the scene – his car, his coat, his day! An effective photograph reveals the character of the subject. In this series, I see confidence and self-assurance.

□ Photography

To capture the fast action, quick focus was needed, so I chose the Nikon 8008s with the 80-200mm lens. Natural light and real action combine to depict a small part in the story of the day. This is true photojournalistic style, capturing the action as it happens – anticipating where the action will be, and being there. To capture these fleeting moments you need to move, look, react immediately to what is happening. To shoot this series, I chose Royal Gold 400 for its beautiful color and fine grain structure.

□ Psychology

I try to put myself into my subject's mind. This helps me to predict where the subject will go and what he will do.

"An effective photograph reveals the character of the subject."

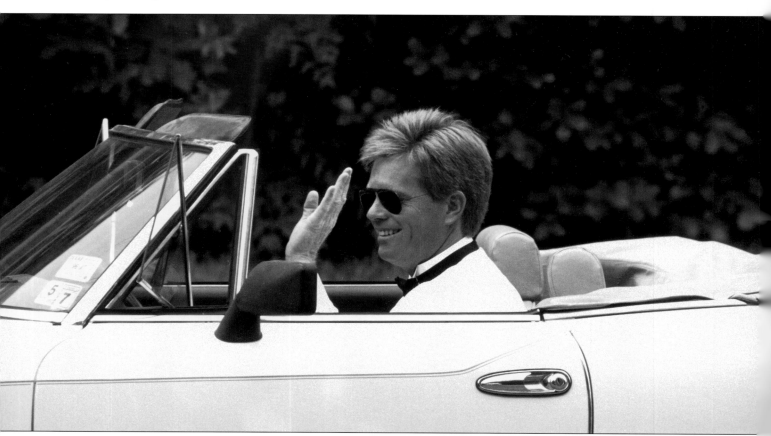

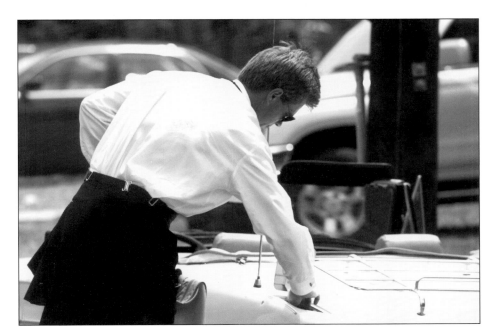

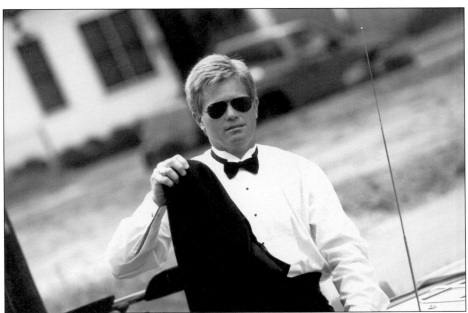

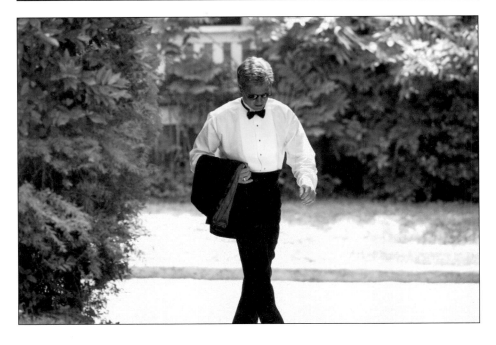

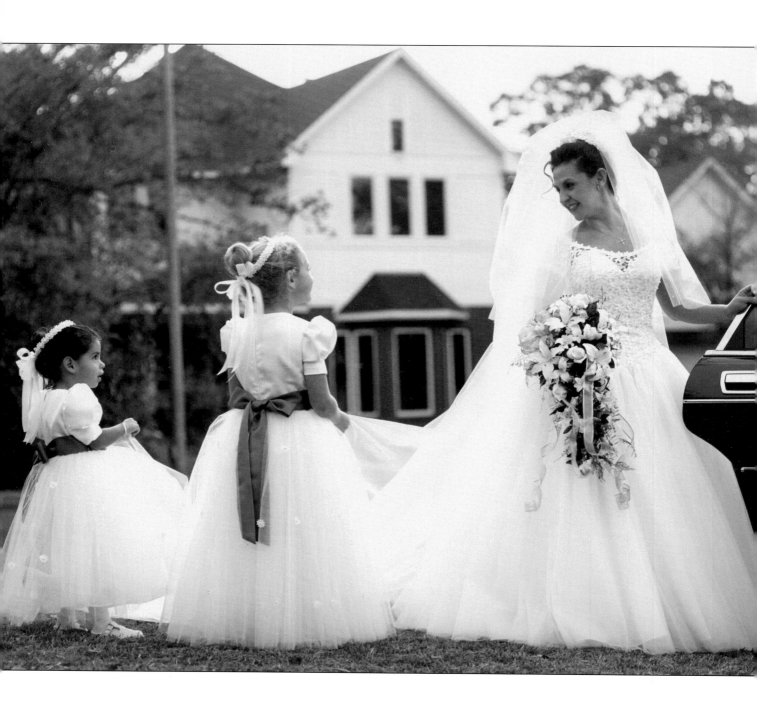

"I 'loosely' placed the girls and talked them through a series of images..."

□ Pose

I have to admit that I set this up, because the wedding was scheduled to begin after dark. If we had taken this image when the ceremony actually took place, there would have been no natural light. For this reason, we planned ahead of time to come by the bride's home and do some images with her, the flower girls, and her family. I believe it's important to take the time to make an image feel as genuine as possible. I "loosely" placed the girls and talked them through a series of images as they held the dress and talked with the bride.

□ Props and Background

The car and the dress are the props. The bride had a long veil and two special young ladies to help her manage it. I needed to capture that and felt that the natural light made for a better image than an electronic flash would have. To add a personal touch to the photograph, I made her neighborhood the setting for this image.

□ Photography

I chose the 120mm lens to give some compression to the image and reduce the sky as much as possible while still allowing me to work closely in a small area. I used a low camera angle for two reasons: to block out some of the houses and the road in the background, and also because of the small stature of the little girls. The low camera angle gives you the feeling of being on their level and seeing the world from their view point.

□ Psychology

I often talk to people rather than direct them. A storytelling conversation brings out natural actions from people. Comments like "Can you help the bride get into the car?" and "Look how pretty she looks!" can elicit movements, expressions and emotions that traditional posing would never evoke. Simply placing the girls and telling them to stand and look at the bride would not give us realistic images. When viewing the scene, think of shapes, contrasts, lighting and backgrounds that will accurately convey the feelings your clients are looking for.

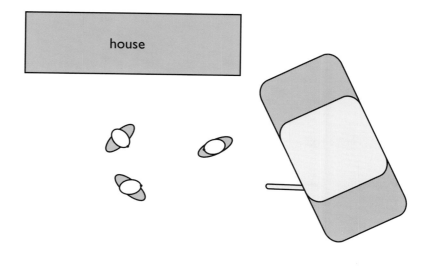

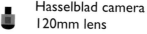
Hasselblad camera
120mm lens

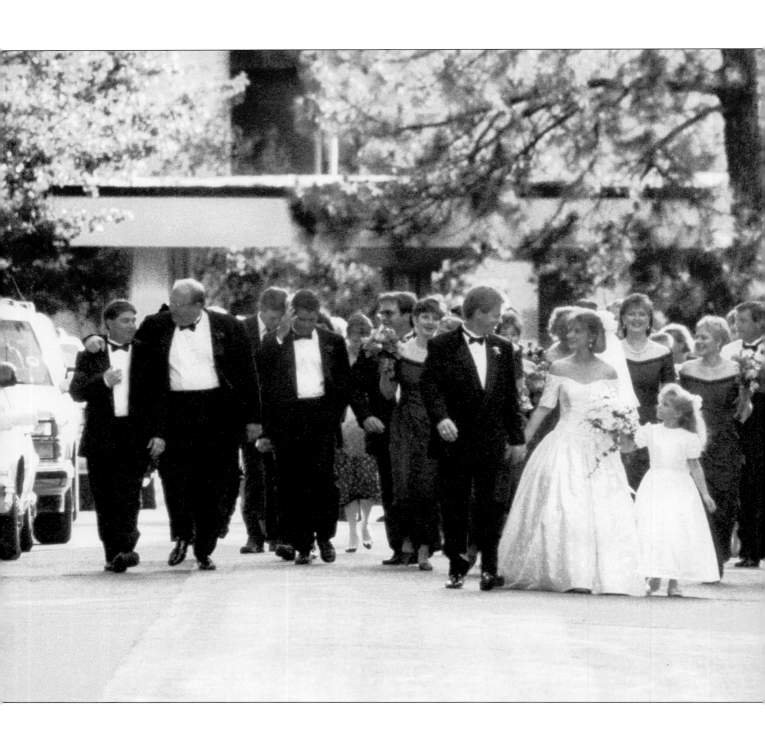

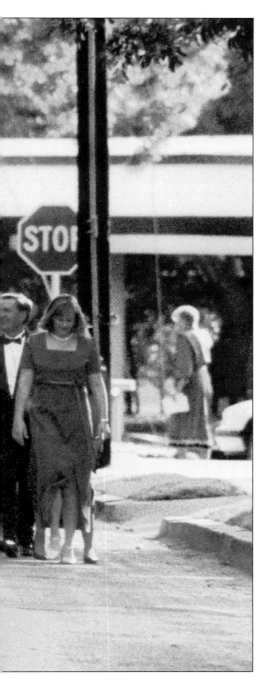

□ Pose

This was the idea of the bride's father. The reception was at the bride's home, a few blocks away from the church. Since the parking around the house was limited, the bridal party and the guests walked to the reception. It made for a fun image that we used as a two-page panoramic print in the album. Look closely at what is happening in this image. It is not just a snapshot of people walking down the street. Look at the bride, the groom and the flower girl (his daughter). This image shows the love they have for each other. It shows the fun they are having in this "journey" on their wedding day. Look at the light shining on the bride's veil and groom's hair. I can't take credit for the light, but I can for the timing of the image. Also notice the two groomsmen on the far left. They are friends, maybe friends who haven't seen each other in a while, and their stance captures the relationship. Watch for little things that make your images special.

□ Photography

I used the Nikon 8008s on this shot, and the 300mm lens. It was set on program mode and auto-focus continuous mode. I left the 1000 speed film in the camera that I had used during the ceremony because I wanted the grain of the fast film to add to a feeling that the camera was some distance from the action.

□ Psychology

Again, capture the story. Capture the action, as it happens. This was a special event in the day. I would have been remiss had I not recorded this moment.

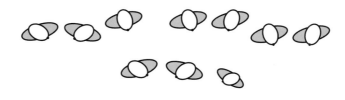

Nikon 8008s camera
300mm lens

☐ Pose

The top image was made as the bride was getting in the carriage. I enjoy the way the young lady is reaching down to pick up her dress as the groom and driver help. Being prepared for pivotal moments will help you capture images like this as they happen. This type of image is much more realistic than those where the subjects are posed, smiling and looking at the camera. There are several different approaches to making wedding images: photojournalistic (where you attempt to document events as they happen); traditional (where you control or pose the subjects in the image); and a combination of the two. This last approach involves the photographer placing the subjects in a particular place and either allowing the subjects to naturally pose themselves or subtly coaxing them into situating themselves for beautiful images. This method was used in the creation of the lower image here. Since subject placement can change the mood of any image, I chose to situate the subjects in the lower right hand corner of the photograph to add to the feeling of privacy and intimacy.

☐ Prop

The horse drawn carriage, complete with a driver decked out in a top hat, was a central focus of the day. The bride arrived at the outdoor ceremony in it, the newlyweds rode to the reception in it, the driver gave rides to the guests at the reception, and the bride and groom eventually departed in it.

☐ Background

The upper image has a light, airy feel. The open sky balances with the white dress and light colored horse. In the lower photograph, the thick trees and native wild flowers in the foreground add to the natural feel. The relationship of the prop to the background and the subject to the background adds to the overall emotional content of each image. The lower image also works well as a panoramic. Cover the top of the image to see the long, slim rendition.

☐ Photography

The image of the carriage was made with a 50mm lens on my Hasselblad. What made this image possible was being in the right place at the right time. Learn to anticipate the action. Don't attempt to go where the action is – go to where the action will be. The lower image was made with the 250mm lens. I think what makes this image special is the subject placement. The couple are in the lower 1/3 of the image and off center. This adds to the feeling of the relative smallness of the couple compared to the large trees and open, natural setting.

☐ Psychology

Both of these images capture the dreams of the bride. As most women realize, the wedding is a culmination of years and years of dreams of what this special day will be like. Your job as photographer or storyteller is to capture this day the way she dreamed it would be. Two important steps towards doing this are asking questions and being a good listener.

"Being prepared for pivotal moments will help you capture images like this as they happen."

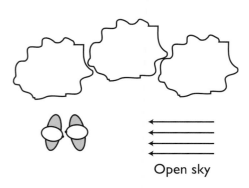

Open sky

■ Hasselblad camera
■ 250mm lens

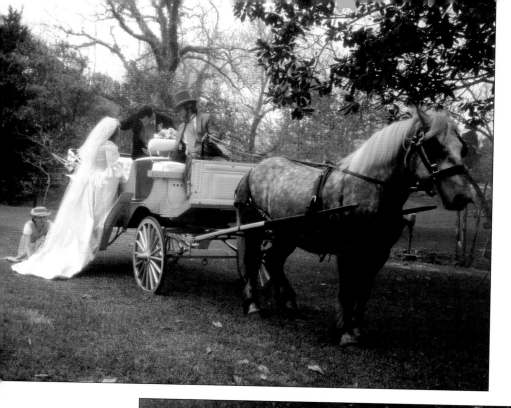

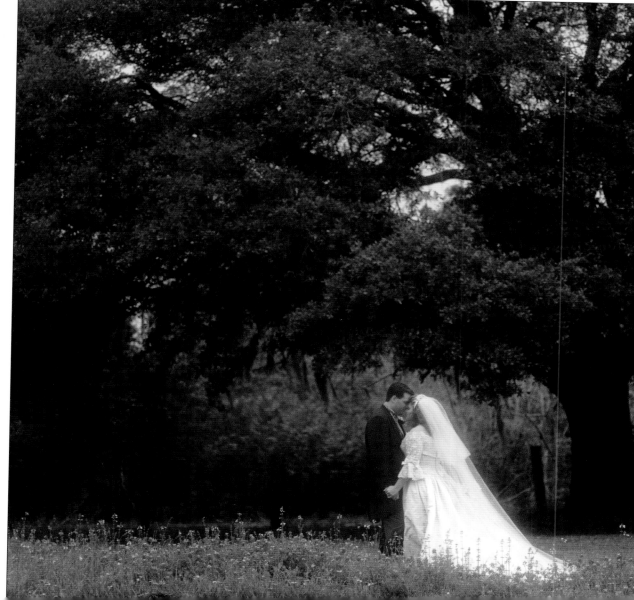

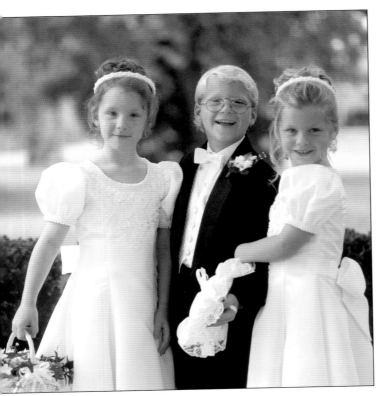

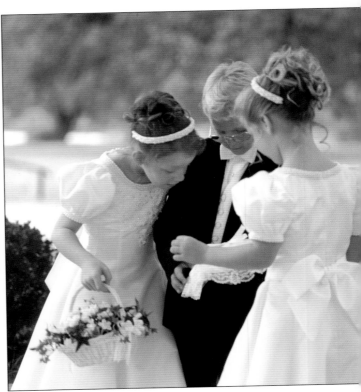

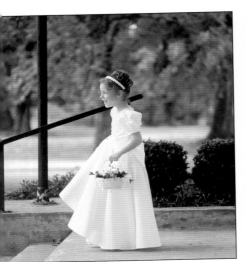

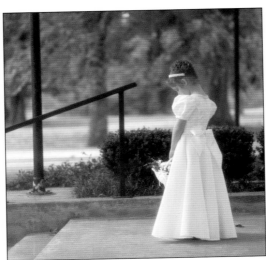

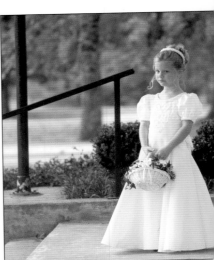

"The wonderment of children is one of my favorite parts of wedding photography."

☐ Pose

I brought the children together in an area that would give me soft but directional light. "What does he have on that pillow?" I playfully asked. "Can you get the rings off?" Look at the natural action of the image on the top right. While I had them together, progressing to the portrait style images was a natural step. The wonderment of children is one of my favorite parts of wedding photography. Children make a wedding special; their innocence and happiness add to the joy of the day.

☐ Background

It was just starting to sprinkle, so I had to work fast. A huge live oak tree provided the directional outdoor light. The canopy blocked the light from the top and protected us from the light rain. The church to the right blocked the light from that direction.

☐ Photography

Notice how nicely the background is thrown completely out of focus in the group shots. The 250mm lens and wide open aperture makes this possible. I used Kodak PPF film (1/30 at f-5.6) and a tripod to eliminate camera movement. A good rule of thumb for deciding when to use a tripod is to put a one over the focal length of the lens make that the minimum speed at which you can hand hold the camera steadily. In this instance, I would have needed a 1/250 second shutter speed (1 over 250 [250mm lens] = 1/250) to reliably hand hold the camera. The low light situation dictated that I use a tripod.

☐ Psychology

A trick that I use to mesmerize children and almost always get a beautiful, natural expression comes from a friend of mine, Don Barnes from Denton, Texas. I take a quarter and push it firmly against my forehead. It will stick there for a while. This seems to work best on oily skin. Then I ask the children to blow it off. When they blow, I raise my eyebrows in a surprised look. The act of raising my eyebrows wrinkles my forehead and causes the quarter to fall. I catch it in my hand and start the whole process over. "Don't blow yet!" I tell them. "Is it still there?" I question. All this time, they tend to supply some truly memorable expressions. After they "blow it off," I almost always get a great smile. Usually I see the children trying to get a quarter to stick to their forehead for the rest of the day. It won't work for them, so they come back to me to see it work again. Thanks Don!

The one piece of advice I can share with you about working with children is be ready! The cute little red head in the lower images changed her mood in a split second, and I was there to capture this transformation as it happened.

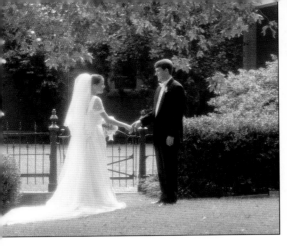
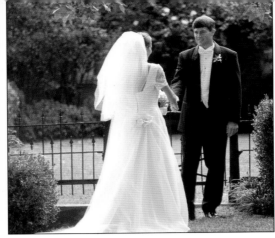
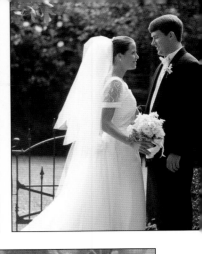
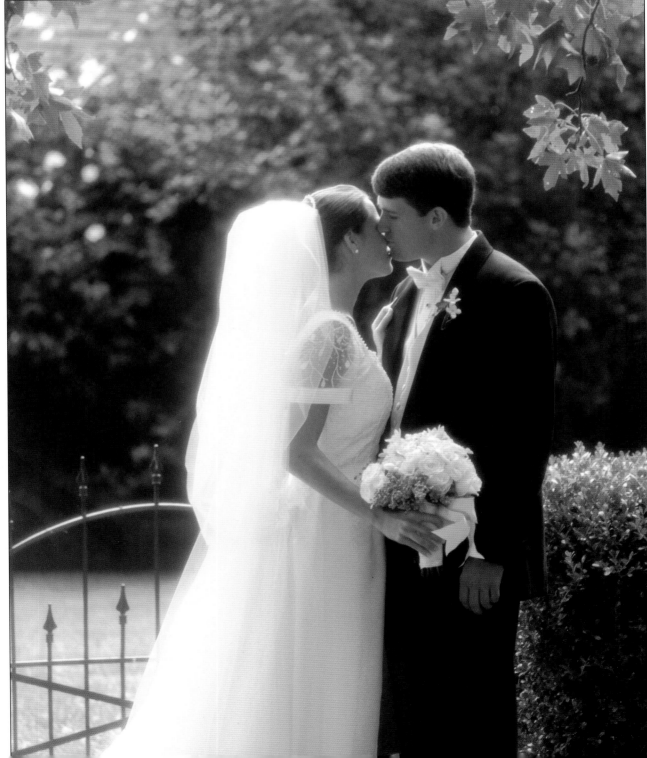

"This series of images almost looks like frames from a movie..."

□ **Pose**

This series of images almost looks like frames from a movie: a spontaneous movement toward each other, reaching for a hand, and a gentle kiss.

□ **Background**

The beautiful garden area in which the image was shot is located just outside the sanctuary. There was a patch of open sky above and behind the couple that added the soft rim light to the images.

□ **Photography**

The 250mm lens (my favorite portrait lens) isolates the subjects from the background. I used a soft focus filter in two of the images to enhance their dream-like quality.

□ **Psychology**

I believe that the photographer's personality is at least 50% of what makes a wedding photographer great. How does the photographer work with the wedding party? Will he/she be polite and friendly with the guests? Can he/she read the people and know how to get the images you want without being pushy? Can the photographer work well with children? The biggest problem with communicating one's personality is that it is hard to convey it to prospective clients. I believe if you look closely, you can see the personality of the photographer in the image. If the subjects look natural and comfortable, it is probably because the photographer made the people feel relaxed.

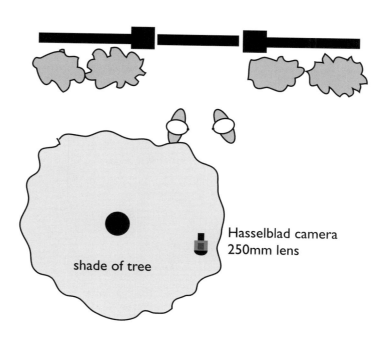

Hasselblad camera
250mm lens

shade of tree

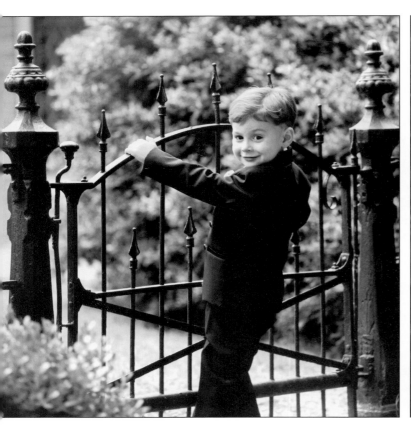

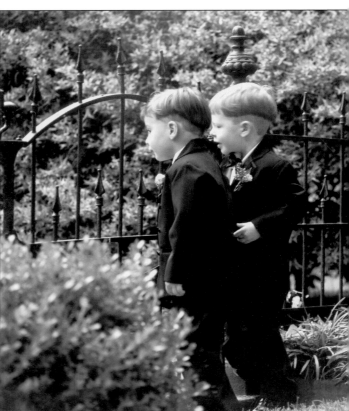

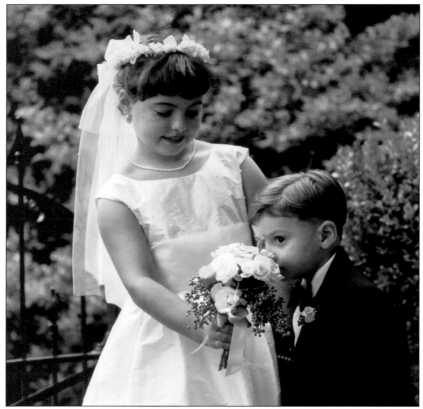

"You can't get these types of images posing little boys."

□ Pose

You can't get these types of images posing little boys. Children are naturally inquisitive, so use their curiosity. Let them be themselves, but give them gentle direction. "Those flowers smell like candy – can you smell the candy?" "What's in there?" or "Are you supposed to climb on that fence?" are questions that can bring out the beautiful personality in children. But be ready, as moments like these don't last long.

□ Prop

These images were made in a small garden next to the church. The beautiful gate makes a wonderful prop and adds another memory to the bride's album. This is her church, and the garden has a special meaning for her.

□ Photography

I used the 250mm lens in these images for two reasons. It limits the scope of the background (due to the small angle of view) and throws the background out of focus (because of the limited depth of field). The long focal length also lets you work at a greater distance from the subjects, allowing the children to be more spontaneous. There is light from an open sky coming from the garden area at camera left which supplied the directional quality of the light. The film used was Kodak PPF ISO 400.

□ Psychology

Realism is an important part of story-telling wedding photography. Sometimes you have to encourage people because they are nervous or uncomfortable. One of the beautiful things about weddings is that everyone is in a good mood and having fun. My job is to record the story for the bride and groom (along with their family and friends) to enjoy for years to come.

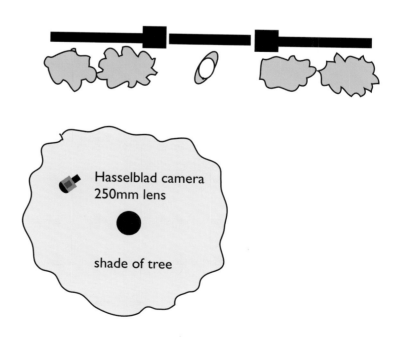

Hasselblad camera
250mm lens

shade of tree

□ Pose

It is no doubt rare that you would catch flowergirls on their front porch and holding their bouquets. What if this doesn't happen naturally? You can encourage it by talking to them in an inquisitive way. Saying something like, "Do you want to go inside?" or "What are they doing in there?" can inspire the natural behavior that produces this kind of priceless moment.

□ Prop/Background

The door to the house is both the prop and the background. It is also part of the illustrative quality of the image.

□ Photography

The photography couldn't be simpler – a good camera (Hasselblad), good film (Kodak) and a quick eye. The soft sun of late afternoon provides a beautiful quality of light.

□ Psychology

One of the things I feel brides want from a wedding photographer is "peace of mind." Once they hire you, they don't want to have to worry about photography. That becomes exclusively your responsibility. Your experience, your style, your "eye" and your personality are the things they want from you. Talk to the bride and groom before the wedding to discover their vision of how they would like the wedding to be photographed. Then use your experience and training to tell the story of the day the way they would like to see it told.

> "You can encourage it by talking to them in an inquisitive way."

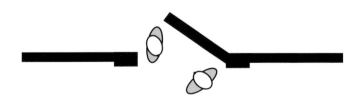

■ Hasselblad camera
250mm lens

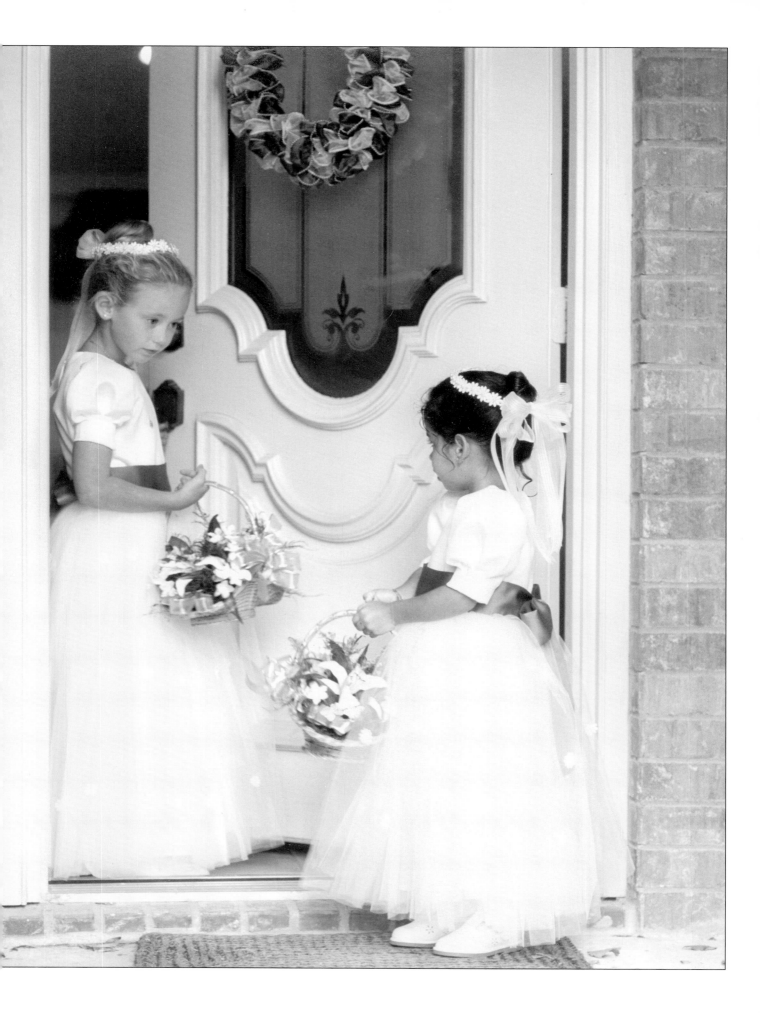

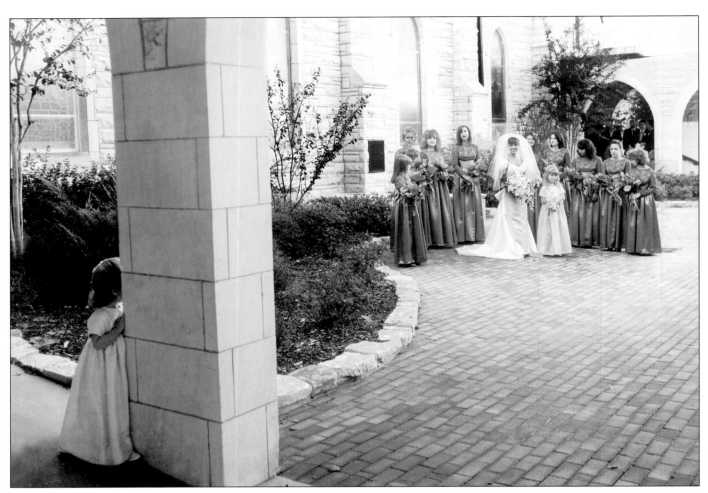

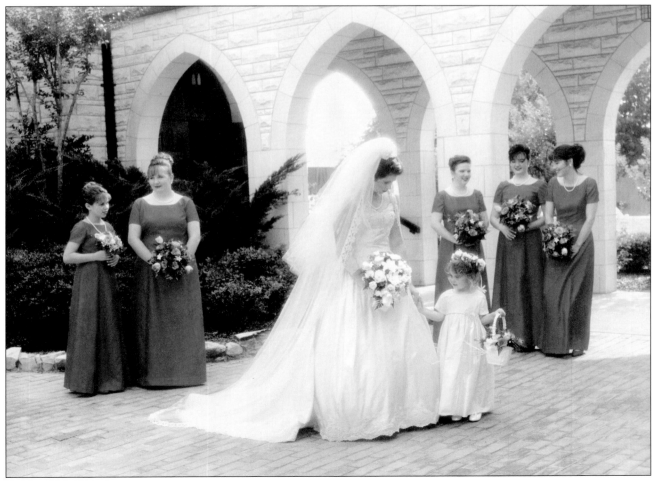

"I try to create interest, depth and a feeling of spontaneity."

☐ Pose

Two versions of a similar image are presented here. The image on the bottom was posed. When I pose groups, I try to create interest, depth and a feeling of spontaneity. I brought the bride and flower girl forward to create a sense of separation from the rest of the group.

In the upper image, notice the little flower girl on the left. She did not want to cooperate for photographs. We tried to get her to join in, but she would have nothing to do with being in the images. Yet, she always wanted to see what was going on. I noticed her hiding behind the post and told the bride and bridesmaids to stay put while I snuck around behind her to capture this priceless moment. This is a good example of how patience and ingenuity can result in an honest representation of "real life." This image never fails to invoke a smile or a chuckle.

☐ Background

As you can see, both images were taken at the same church. This courtyard has arches on three sides. One of the sides always offers great light, making it a beautiful place in which to take photographs.

☐ Photography

Both images were made with the 50mm lens using my Hasselblad camera and Kodak Pro 400 film in available light. This wide angle lens has great depth of field, allowing almost everything in the image to be in focus. It also exaggerates depth and accents the foreground.

☐ Psychology

Both images are representative of a small chapter in the bride's wedding storybook. I realistically captured moments in a way that reflects the true nature and spirit of her wedding day.

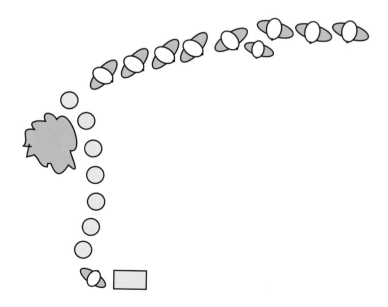

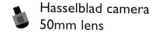

Hasselblad camera
50mm lens

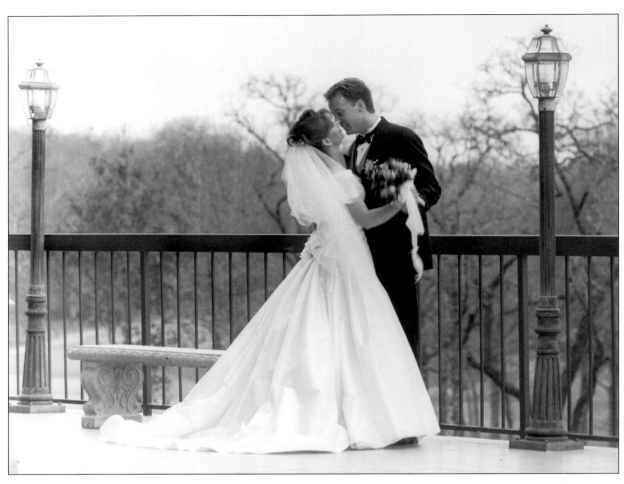

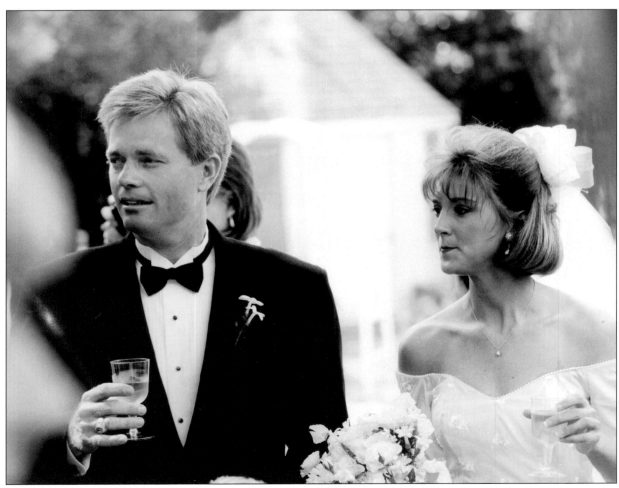

"... spontaneous moments should be a big part of wedding coverage."

□ Pose

These and other spontaneous moments should be a big part of wedding coverage. Many photographers don't include extemporaneous images in their wedding coverage because they require more precision. You have to be ready all the time and able to anticipate the action.

□ Photography

The bottom image was made with the Nikon 8008s camera, 80-200mm zoom lens set on 200mm using TMZ 3200 film. It was made right after a toast. Look at the expression on the bride; you can see her reaction to the champagne. I love the way this image "looks through" a group of people.

The top image was shot with a 250mm lens on the Hasselblad camera using Kodak Pro 400 film. It was taken on the porch of the Pebble Creek Country Club, a beautiful facility where I have shot weddings many times. When I am working here, I try to get the couple to go out on the porch right before sunset. The light at that time of the day is beautiful.

□ Psychology

I've found that brides don't want you to take them away from their guests. They want beautiful images, but they don't want to spend the day being photographed away from their friends and family. Learning to make these spontaneous images fulfills your need to capture great images and the bride's need to be with her guests. Watch the bride and groom with camera ready. Watch the bride through the camera. When you do take the couple away from their guests, be respectful and work quickly. Plan your images and do your best to orchestrate the time efficiently. Don't keep the couple away from friends and family more than a few minutes at a time.

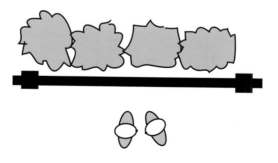

Hasselblad camera
250mm lens

□ Pose

The bride and groom came out on the porch for a few minutes to let me create some images. I asked the bride to sit down on the edge of the bench and told the groom to "just go over and be beside your new bride." He naturally took her hand and leaned on the rail. Then I backed up and let them spend a few minutes alone. Your job is to give them subtle directions like "Both of you look over towards the building," or "Give each other a hug." Then you can make small adjustments like moving a hand or tilting a head without orchestrating the photograph too much.

□ Prop

Some people feel more comfortable with something in their hands. For the bride, the bouquet is perfect. She can hold it, place it beside her or bring it up close to be part of the image. This groom was having a drink when we went outside. He brought it with him, and it gave a natural look to the photograph.

□ Background

The trees and the golf course are the overall background. The railing and the lamp posts are the middle ground and add a nice feel to the image. I stood on another bench to bring the skyline above the heads of the couple. I feel one of the little things that separates a true professional from "just another wedding photographer" is being aware of the background. This would not have been as good an image if the skyline ran right through the couple's heads. In an image like this, you could even crop the white sky out completely.

□ Photography

The 250mm lens, a meter and a tripod were all that I needed to capture this available light image. I use the Bogen 2031 tripod and the hand grip at weddings. It is lightweight, and will position the camera anywhere from 18" off the ground to 7' in the air. Remember, when using a lightweight tripod and slow shutter speeds, a cable release will help you to avoid camera shake.

□ Psychology

For most brides, this day is the culmination of years of plans and dreams. It is a fantasy come true. My responsibility is to capture this occasion the way she envisioned it. She wants her pictures to look as beautiful as she expected this day to be. You can play a large part in helping her fulfill her dream.

"I backed up and let them spend a few minutes alone."

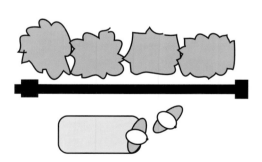

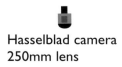

Hasselblad camera
250mm lens

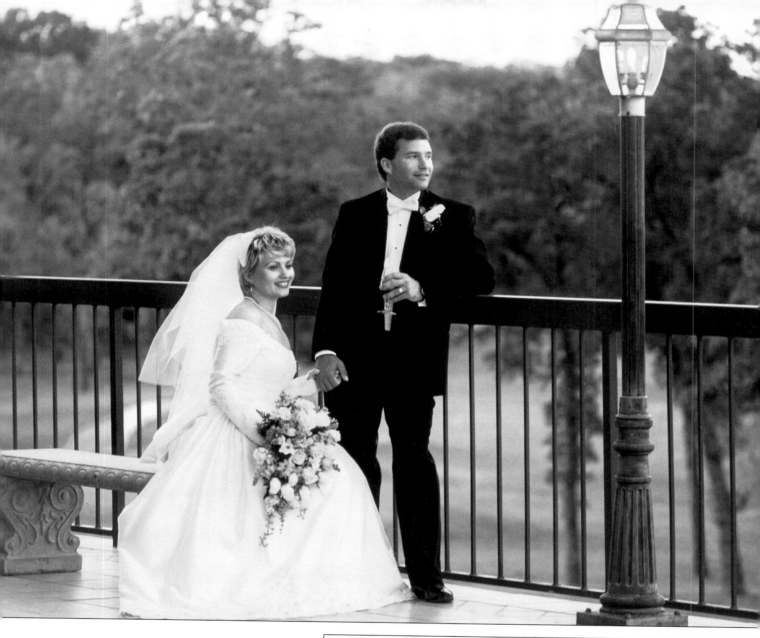
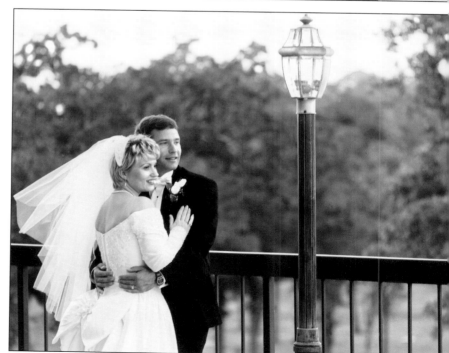

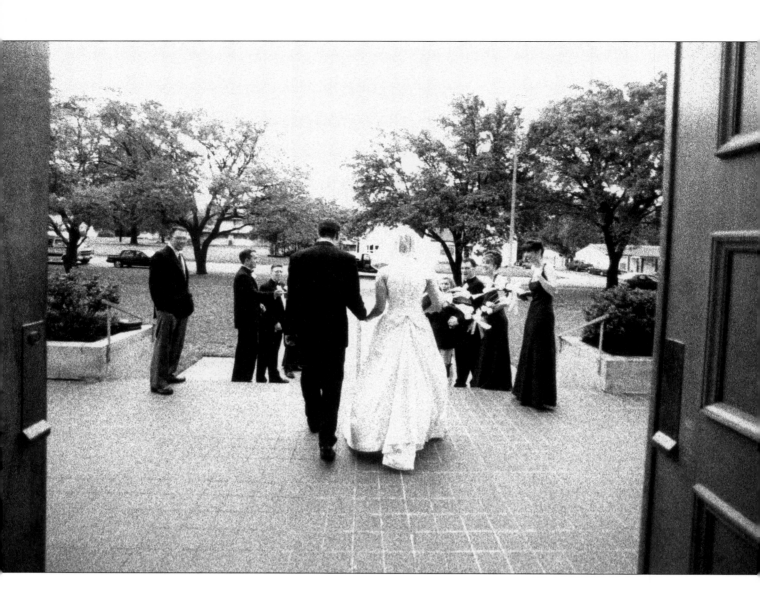

"This is a long-standing dispute among wedding photographers."

□ Pose

Is this posed or completely natural? At some weddings, great spontaneous moments just happen. As a professional, I do my best to capture them. If they are not happening, I feel it is my job to help them happen. This is a long-standing dispute among wedding photographers. Essentially, the question is whether to pose or not to pose. I do both. I make a lot of "photojournalistic" images, just as they happen, but I also coax images that look natural. I feel that being able to suggest or make recommendations to people is a special and valuable talent. Your demeanor and disposition can make or break this situation. Think of weddings as a movie production set where you are the director. At this wedding, there was so much action, most of the images were photographed just as they happened.

□ Props and Background

The doors and the walkway are the props and background. The lines in the door and the doors themselves lead your eye to the subjects, as does the action. Even though you can't see the couple's faces, this image is part of the story. We liked this image so much that we decided to make it a double page panorama in their album.

□ Photography

I am often asked why I use Hasselblad equipment to photograph weddings. There are several reasons. First, I believe it is one of the finest cameras on the market. Second, all of the lenses, backs, prisms and accessories are completely interchangeable, no matter how old your equipment may be. Everything I bought, from the first camera body to the last lens all work together. Third, the equipment is also very rugged. My equipment has been dropped, knocked over, stuffed in a camera bag and even left out in the rain, and it keeps on performing like new. Fourth, it's square! I love square prints. I first decided on a square format because I hated when a bride looked at her album where the prints were not square (both horizontal and vertical images) and the album had to be constantly rotated for the vertical and horizontal images. Fifth, the equipment is compact and lightweight, which is a big advantage for both portrait and wedding photographers. And last but not least, it holds its value better than any camera I have ever owned. Every piece of equipment I have ever bought is worth more than I paid for it. I consider Hasselblad cameras more of a sound investment than a business expense.

□ Psychology

Over the years, we have evolved from a conventional photography studio into a more exciting enterprise. We create fine art quality portraits and wedding albums that have a scenic quality, are emotionally charged and have a natural look with an artistic impression. We call it photojournalism. It is a refreshing new approach to wedding photography. The images have an un-posed, spontaneous and storytelling feel. It takes creative instinct to be able to combine portraiture and photojournalism in a wedding album and still keep everything looking natural.

TWIN LIGHTING

Twin lighting adds dimension to the flowers and clothing, and a portrait quality to your images of people. Use it to put your photography on a different, more upscale level.

"... you will see a marked improvement in your flash photography."

☐ Twin Lighting

Twin lighting (the use of two lights) can be used to add a second dimension to your wedding images. It adds texture to the clothing and flowers and a portrait quality to the photographs. It also creates dimension in your images. The same results usually cannot be achieved with only the on-camera flash.

☐ Main Light

In the next several pages, you will learn several ways to use twin lighting in your wedding photographs. As you will see, sometimes the second light is used as a main light, with the on-camera flash used as a fill light. This is very similar to regular studio lighting.

☐ Accent Light

Sometimes the second light is used as an accent or dimension light. In group photographs, this light skims the subjects, adding texture and dimension to your images. It should not overpower, as the light on the camera is the main light in these situations.

☐ Special Effects Light

Another use for the second light is for special effects. This application is used for impact. It separates your images from run-of-the-mill photographs.

☐ Second Main Light

The last use we will learn for the second light is where it is used as a second main light on secondary subjects. The on-camera flash is also used as a main light, but on the main subject. I use this technique mainly for throwing the garter and bouquet.

If you learn to use twin lighting techniques, you will see a marked improvement in your flash photography. It will also put your photography on a different and upscale level.

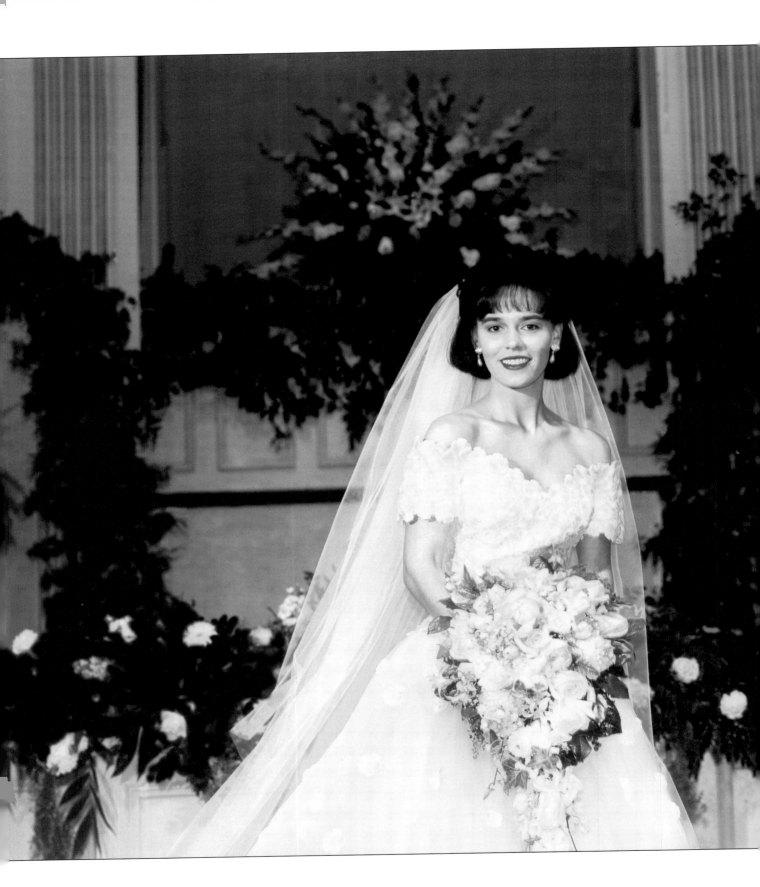

"In this example, the second light is used as a main light."

□ Pose

This is a traditional 3/4 length pose of a beautiful bride. A good pose starts with the feet. Have the bride place her weight on her back foot (the foot farthest from the camera). The front foot should point toward the camera. Have her bend the knee of the front foot and push the knee in slightly. This will cause her back shoulder to drop slightly. You will notice her shoulders are turned slightly away from the camera and her face is turned back in the opposite direction. This is the classic feminine pose which gives a flattering S-curve to her body.

□ Background

The background is the bride's church, and I placed her off-center for added impact.

□ Photography

There are several ways to use a second light. In this example, the second light is used as a main light. The on-camera flash is used as a fill light (see the drawing below). I set the camera between f-5.6 and f-8. The flash on the camera was set at f-5.6 on automatic. The second light, the main light, was set to f-8. The shutter speed was set at 1/15 second to pick up some of the ambient light. This is called dragging the shutter. A faster shutter speed would have caused the background to go darker.

□ Psychology

We combine two different wedding styles, traditional coverage and photojournalistic coverage, and still keep everything natural. The traditional style includes all of the wedding images you have come to expect in a traditional wedding album, including portraits of the bride and groom, attendants, and family as well as the traditional happenings at most weddings. The photojournalistic style is a more realistic style of wedding photography. It includes un-posed, spontaneous photographs during the wedding day. I want to document the events of a wedding, to capture moments with a natural and real feeling to the images. Unlike most photographers, we utilize a combination of the two styles.

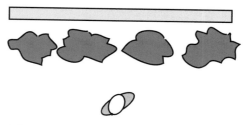

second light at f-8
(used as main light
in this situation)

Quantum
Q-Flash
set on automatic
f-5.6

Hasselblad camera
120mm lens
set between f-5.6 and f-8

☐ Pose

This is another lovely pose for the bride. There are several aspects to notice on this image. First, I shot the image down the aisle instead of at the altar. This minimizes the altar area and puts the emphasis on the bride. Second, this is a very classic pose. Start by placing the feet with the weight on her left foot and with the right foot forward. Her shoulders should be turned at a 45° angle from the background. Position the bride's face in profile (where you see exactly half of her face). Point the flowers down, arm slightly bent and chin up to give separation from the shoulder. For this image, I dragged the shutter to balance the background with the subject.

☐ Background

The background is quite separated from the subject. The background brightness is balanced with the subject by the shutter speed. Because this church has almost no windows or natural light, the background, lit by incandescent light, provides a warm glow. The bows which adorn the pews lead your eyes to the bride. Some would argue that the bows are distracting; I disagree, as these bows were a part of the decorations and a decorative element that the bride chose for her special day.

☐ Photography

Twin lighting is a big part of what makes this image noteworthy. In this case, the second light is the main light. It is set one to two stops brighter than the fill light (the on-camera flash). You must decide how much contrast you prefer. As mentioned above, I dragged the shutter to balance the subject and background. One way to think of dragging the shutter is to consider the subject and the background as two separate images that are combined. The flash is controlled by the f-stop. The shutter speed technically does not affect the subject or the flash. The brightness of the background is controlled by the shutter speed. This was photographed at 1/15 second because I did not want the background to be too bright.

☐ Psychology

One of the frustrations of wedding photography is that almost *every* image is a compromise. If you use two lights, you could use three and include a light behind the bride turned toward the camera to light the veil. If three is good, would four not be better? For instance, a kicker light positioned about fifteen feet back and to the left skimming off the back of the bride? What about two lights lighting the background? What about a spot light on the cross? Stop! Remember that you only have a few minutes to do a few dozen images. Also keep in mind that this is not just a photo session; there is a wedding going on here! Your job is to do the best you can with the limited amount of time allowed. Twin lighting can be done with relatively little extra time. I feel that it adds another dimension to your photography. Twin lighting takes your photography to the next level. If I am without twin lighting at a wedding, I feel I am not doing everything I can for the bride.

"This is another classic pose for the bride."

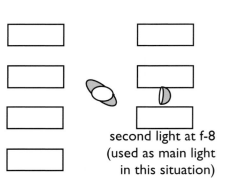

second light at f-8
(used as main light
in this situation)

Quantum
Q-Flash
set on
automatic
f-5.6

Hasselblad
camera
120mm lens
set at f-8

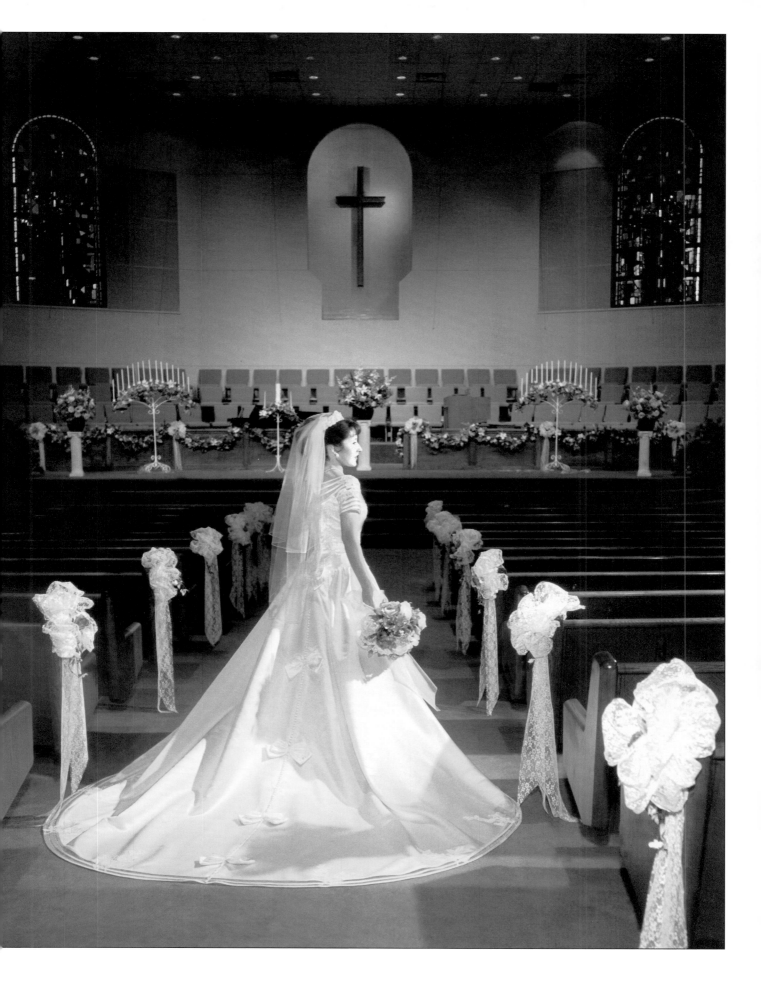

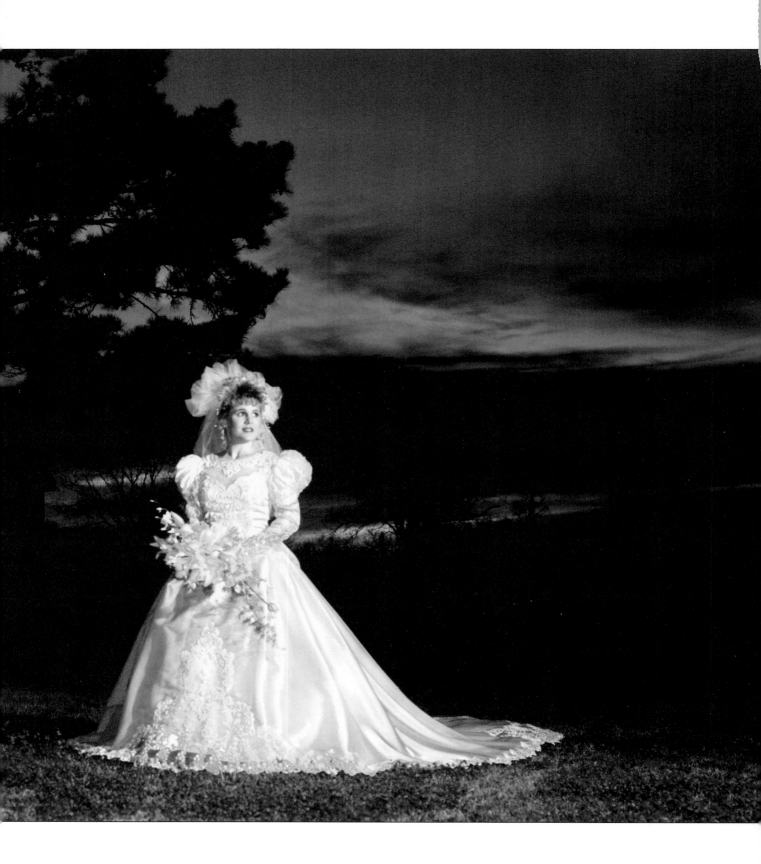

"This image will remind her of one part of the beautiful story that was her wedding day."

☐ Pose

Always start with the feet. Have the bride put her weight on the back foot, with the front foot forward pointing at the camera. Her shoulders should be turned away from the camera and her face turned back in the other direction. In this image, I chose to do a 2/3 view of the face.

☐ Background

As we were leaving the church, I noticed the gorgeous sunset and envisioned a great image. This image will remind her of one part of the beautiful story that was her wedding day.

☐ Photography

Twin lighting is used again. Here, the second light (off-camera light) is used as the main light. The on-camera flash is the fill light. The sunset is balanced to the subject with the shutter speed. The camera was set on f-8, the main light at f-8, fill light f-5.6, shutter speed 1/30 second. Although you can't control the brightness of the sun, you do have complete control over how your camera will record the brightness of the sunset. The faster the shutter speed, the darker the sunset will appear in the image; the slower the shutter speed, the brighter the sunset will appear. I chose this speed because it captured the sunset the way it looked to me. There are a few ways to determine the shutter speed/f-stop combination. One is to use a spot meter. Read the middle tones of the sunset and use the reading on the meter. A second way is to use a Polaroid back on your camera. One of the many advantages of the Hasselblad camera is that you can take the regular film back off and put on a Polaroid back. This way you are testing the exposure through the same lens and with the lighting setup just the way the film will react. A third way is to bracket your exposures. Bracketing is the process of making several exposures, each one at a different setting to determine in what ways each image will be different. When you develop these exposures, you can see what effect each setting had and choose the one that best suits your needs. It would have made the image look better if I had instructed the bride to look more toward her right. This would have centered her eyes in their sockets and shown less of the whites of her eyes.

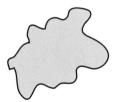

second light at f-8
(used as main light
in this situation)

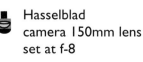

Quantum
Q-Flash
set on automatic
f-5.6

Hasselblad
camera 150mm lens
set at f-8

☐ Pose

I didn't intend for this image to turn out the way it appears here. As I was preparing to do the "back profile" of the bride, I told the groom to relax for a moment. He moved off to the right (to the position shown in the photograph), which was not quite out of the scene. Rather than shoo him farther away, I decided to capture the moment as it happened rather than the way I had planned it. I knew I could get him in the image, but that the main light would not illuminate him sufficiently. The on-camera flash (fill light) would provide some light. However, he would appear darker than the foreground where his bride stood. This was not what I had originally envisioned, but it worked in a different yet equally pleasing way. In fact, what I like most in this image is the fact that the newlyweds appear in the same shot but the lighting defines the bride as the primary subject and the groom as the secondary subject.

☐ Background

The background is the altar at the church. It was an evening ceremony, so I used a 1/30 second shutter speed to keep the background somewhat dark. If I had used a slower shutter speed, the interior wall behind the altar would have recorded lighter and seemed out of key for a wedding at this time of day.

☐ Photography

The twin lighting technique utilizes the lights as you would in the studio. The second light is the main light, while the light on-camera flash is the fill light. I set the fill light on automatic at f-4, two stops below the main light to produce a more dramatic image. One of the best things about the system that I use is that you can quickly change the contrast of the scene by changing the output of the on-camera flash. This can be very useful since, at weddings, you typically don't have a lot of extra time to work with. My wedding photography experiences have led me to the conclusion that time is far more precious than film. Instead of taking the time to test the exact exposure combination you want for each and every image with Polaroid film or precise metering, make several exposures where each has a different contrast level. Start with the main light and the fill light set at the same output (my main light is set on manual — the fill light on the camera is set on automatic). Then make a series of photographs, progressively increasing the differential between the output of the fill and main lights. On consecutive photographs, I change the output of the fill light by setting the f-stop one stop lower. The greater the difference between the two lights, the broader the range of brightness in the image.

"I didn't intend for this image to turn out the way it appears here."

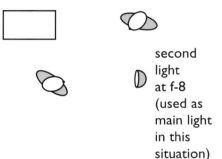

second light at f-8 (used as main light in this situation)

Quantum Q-Flash set on automatic f-4

Hasselblad camera 150mm lens set at f-8

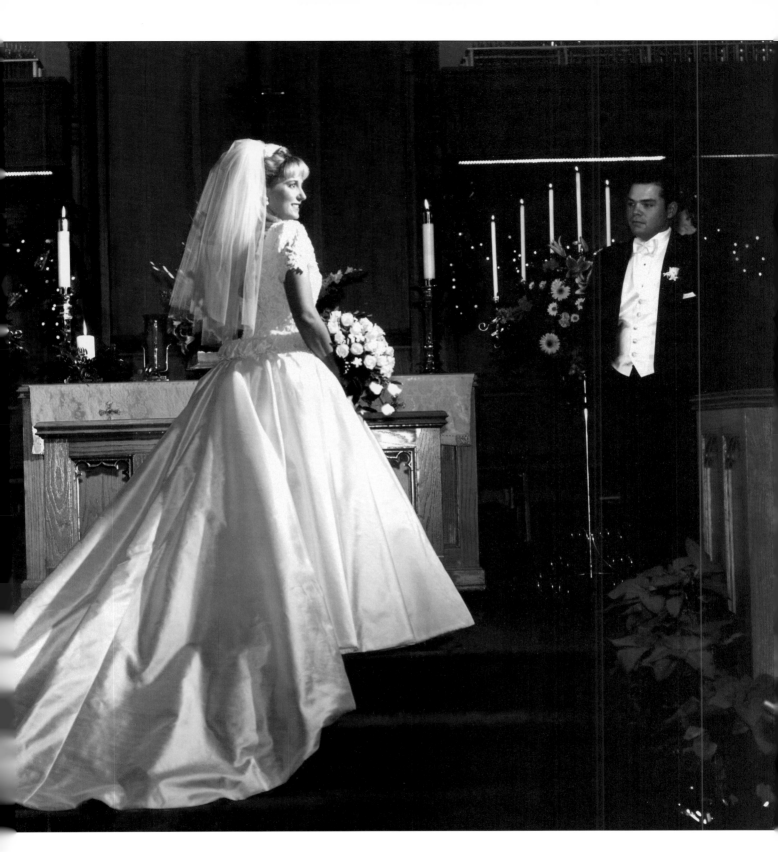

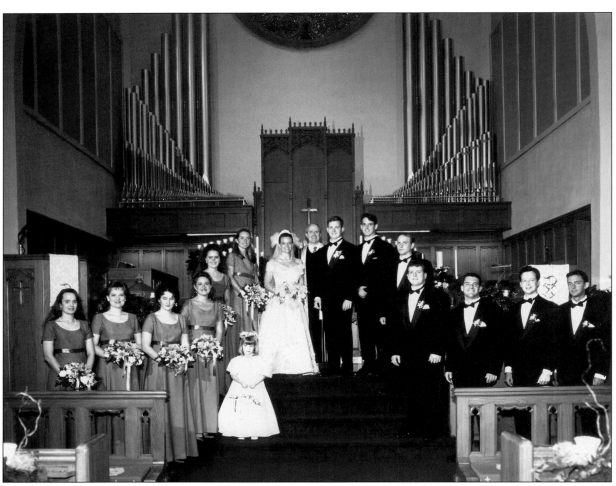

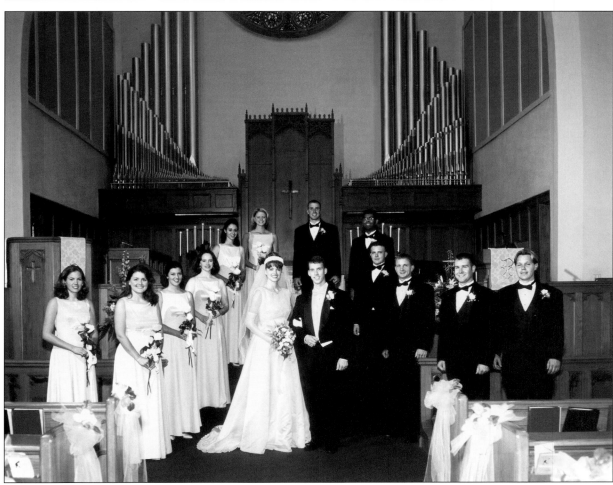

"Have the wedding party turn slightly towards the center..."

☐ Pose

Here is an example of two ways to pose wedding parties. In the top image, the bride and groom are at the top of the steps, with the bridesmaids and groomsmen lined diagonally down each side. In the lower image, I placed the newlyweds down at the bottom of the steps. Both of these images feature the bridesmaids on one side and the groomsmen on the other. This is the way the brides had the wedding parties stand during their respective wedding ceremonies, so that's the way I posed them. But being the photographer means that you decide which looks better. Here you must judge whether placing the couple at the top of the stairs or down front is more effective. Have the wedding party turn slightly towards the center, placing their weight on their back feet (in this instance, the right foot for the guys and left foot for the ladies). Have the groomsmen drop their hands by their sides, ensuring a uniform look.

☐ Photography

For this twin lighting set-up, the off-camera light is an accent (second) light. The light on the camera is the main light. The off-camera light is at a lower power setting than the main light, causing it to lightly skim across the group. One of the problems photographers encounter when first using twin lighting for photographing groups is that they often have the power level of the second light set too high. Start with this light at two stops less than the main light (on-camera). I use the plain reflector, with diffuser, on both strobes. The second light should be raised as high as the light stand will go, approximately six feet to the left and six feet in front of the camera.

☐ Psychology

This is one of the many times, as a photographer, where you need to simultaneously utilize the skills of working fast and reading people. You need to keep their minds off being in front of the camera, as most people are uncomfortable with having their photograph taken. Talk to the group, joke with them while getting them to do what you need them to do. Coming across as a nice guy while keeping things moving along is a talent you need to develop to become a great wedding photographer.

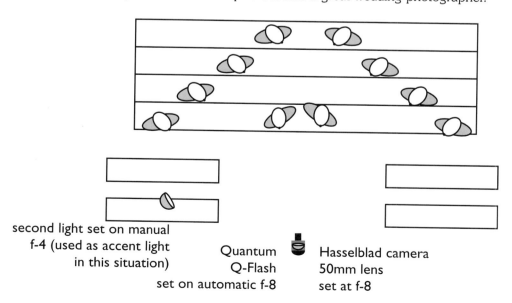

second light set on manual f-4 (used as accent light in this situation)

Quantum Q-Flash set on automatic f-8

Hasselblad camera 50mm lens set at f-8

□ Pose

While leaving the church for the reception, I quickly stopped the couple for about two minutes to make these images, and brought them together in the right place in relationship to the light. I suggested they hold each other, and that's all it took. They just naturally posed themselves, and I captured a moment that embodied the beauty of their wedding day.

□ Props and Background

The arch and the light are strikingly dramatic. Some locations virtually ensure a perfect image.

□ Photography

It was dark, so the shutter speed wasn't critical except for the lamps outside the arch. To include those lights, I chose a setting of 1/30 second so they registered but did not overpower the image. The second light in this image was the main light. It was placed behind the outside wall to shine light on the couple's faces. I used the reflector to keep the light off the wall behind them, as well as to give direction to the light. In the bottom image, I turned the on-camera flash off. I prefer this image, as the darkness outside the arch and the light inside the arch direct the eye to the subjects.

□ Psychology

Being the photographer hired to capture all of the details and special moments that the bride has planned can be very difficult. After all, you are the person she is entrusting to capture the most important day of her entire life. How can she possibly choose? You must give her several reasons to choose you out of all the other photographers in your area. To provide the prospective bride with what she wants, you must first know what her needs and desires are. I believe that most brides want to look beautiful, enjoy their magic day, and not have to worry about whether you are capturing all of the details and special moments that make her wedding uniquely special. She wants the story of her wedding told the way she has always imagined it, not the way some photographer (often a stranger) does for every other wedding. Make it your priority to preserve her special day for eternity!

> "I quickly stopped the couple for about two minutes to make these images..."

second light at f-5.6
(used as main light
in this situation)

Quantum Q-Flash
set on automatic f-4
(not used on
bottom image)

Hasselblad camera
50mm lens
set at f-5.6

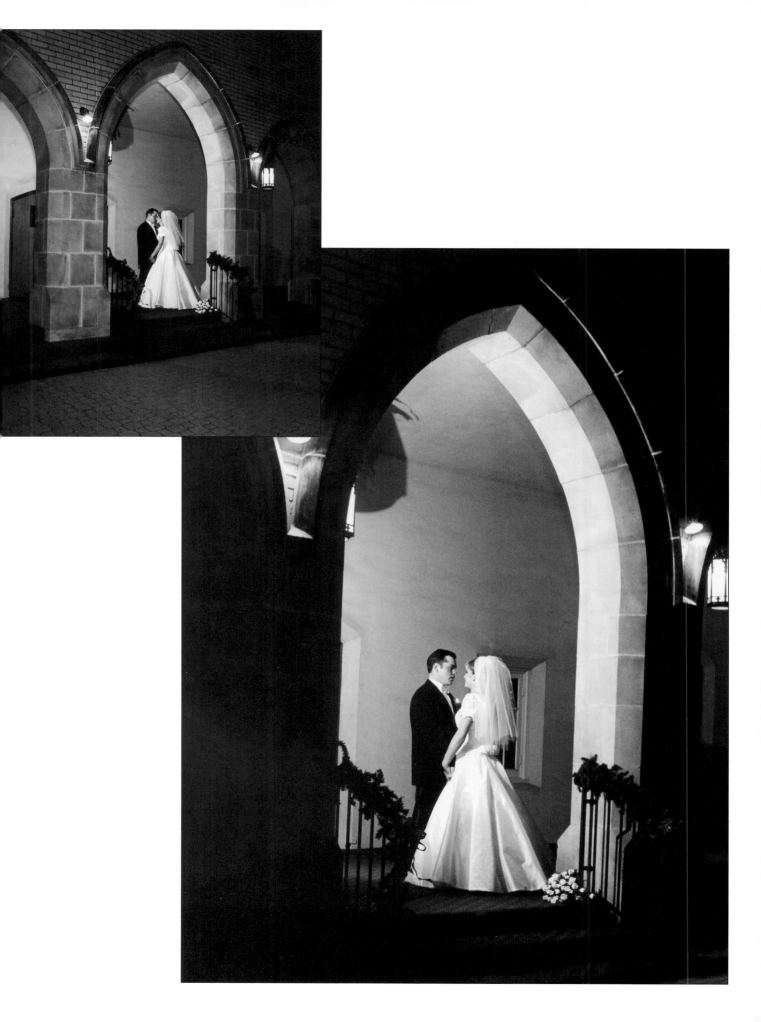

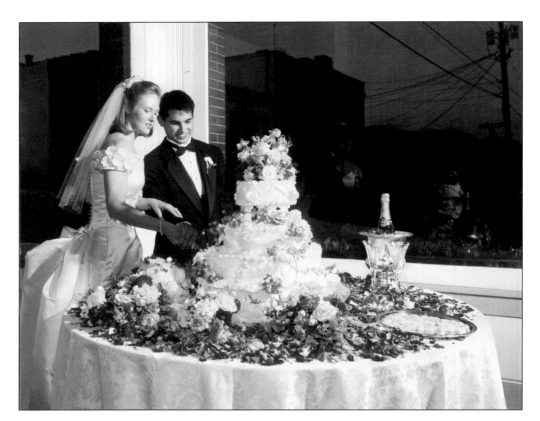

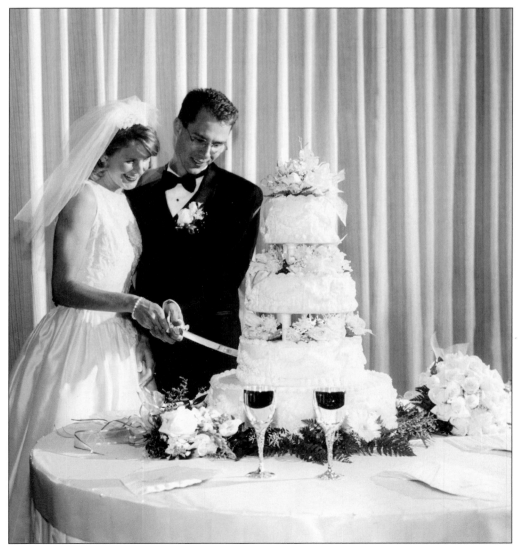

> "... I am sneaky about getting the couple in the right spot without them knowing..."

□ Pose

I basically let the couples cut the cake the way they want, but I am sneaky about getting the couple in the right spot without them knowing that I am placing them in a particular place. I like to place the groom on the side opposite the bride to prevent his arm from "cutting" across her dress. But I also want to see all three of the subjects: the bride, the groom and, of course, the cake. Once I get the couple into a good position, I leave them alone and let them cut.

□ Prop

Naturally, the main prop is the cake. Weddings feature cakes of all kinds, shapes, colors and styles. Plain and detailed, flowered and not, white, ivory, gold – the list goes on and on. Your job is to record the details of the particular cake a given bride has selected. Whether the cake is expensive or homemade, it is special to the couple. Like everything at the wedding, make it look as beautiful as it is (or even better).

□ Background

You typically don't have much choice on the background for shots of the cake – usually the bride or the caterer decides its placement in the reception area. However, you must watch for distractions. Sometimes, moving the camera a few inches can make a big difference in the image. In the upper image, I had to place the flash carefully so it did not reflect in the windows behind the couple.

□ Photography

In this circumstance, the second light has two functions. It is the main light for the bride and groom, and it is an accent light for the cake. Placing the second light around past the cake allows the light to skim over it without becoming overpowering. If you want to start doing twin lighting at weddings, this is a perfect series of images to begin with, since you will usually have time to set up while other activities are going on. I recommend you set up the lights and camera, use a Polaroid back for your camera (if available) and test the set-up before the actual cake-cutting. I would also suggest, at first, that you make exposures both with the second light and without it. I use the Quantum 4i Radio Slave to trigger the second light. One of the features of this unit that makes it perfect for twin lighting are the local and remote switches on the transmitter. You are able to turn on or off either of the lights at the camera without affecting the other light. Never experiment with new techniques at a wedding without first getting the images you need with the techniques you are already familiar with.

□ Education

Having great equipment and great film doesn't guarantee great images. An additional investment in education is crucial. For instance, I have been studying with the top photographers from around the country since 1972. You should join local, state and national photographic associations, and attend meetings whenever you can. The Professional Photographers of America and its affiliates offer week-long schools around the country you can and should attend. Wedding and Portrait Photographers' International is another fine organization. See the supplier list at the end of this book for additional information.

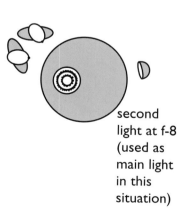

second light at f-8 (used as main light in this situation)

Quantum Q-Flash set on automatic f-5.6

Hasselblad camera 80mm lens set at f-8

□ Lighting and Photography

In this image the second light was used to light up the ice sculpture. As you can see from the image in the lower right-hand corner, without the second light the sculpture is quite bland. I placed the second right up against the sculpture. I used the 50 watt second setting, the lowest setting on the flash. In this instance, the second light (a Lumedyne flash unit) was used for a special effect. I set the camera at f-8, then used the on-camera flash as usual.

The flash I use for my on-camera flash is the Quantum Q flash. I have had excellent results with this flash, as well as with the Quantum Q 4i Electronic slave which has demonstrated great performance. It has local and remote on/off switches, two channels and a high and low speed. I only need one nine volt battery (available anywhere) to power the transmitter, and two nine volt batteries for the receiver. This unit controls both the on-camera flash and the second light. With it, you can trigger either flash independently or simultaneously.

You can also use an optical slave that "sees" the light from one flash, and subsequently triggers the second light. I always carry an optical slave in the camera bag. The problem with this type of trigger is that any flash can trigger it. If someone else makes a flash exposure, the light will go off with his flash.

□ Marketing

One of the most important parts of marketing weddings is to give photographs to the different vendors at the weddings you photograph. After each wedding, make photographs for the flower shop, wedding consultant, bridal store, tuxedo shop, caterer, the country club (or reception area), etc. I sometimes also make photographs of the images of the interior of the sanctuary if the decorations or layout are different than usual, for the place of worship. That way, they can show brides the different ways their location can be set up or decorated. Make sure you sign or stamp the front of these images and place a label on the back with your name, address and phone number. A lot of photographers say they always give photographs to the vendors, but most don't. You can stand out from the crowd by doing it reliably. This is a great way to generate business by ensuring that future brides will see your photographs and your name at every step of planning their wedding. You may also receive referrals from vendors whom brides often ask for advice on selecting a photographer.

> "... without the second light the sculpture is quite bland."

second light at 50 watt seconds
(used as a special effects
light in this situation)

Hasselblad camera
120mm lens
set at f-8

Quantum Q-Flash
set on automatic f-5.6

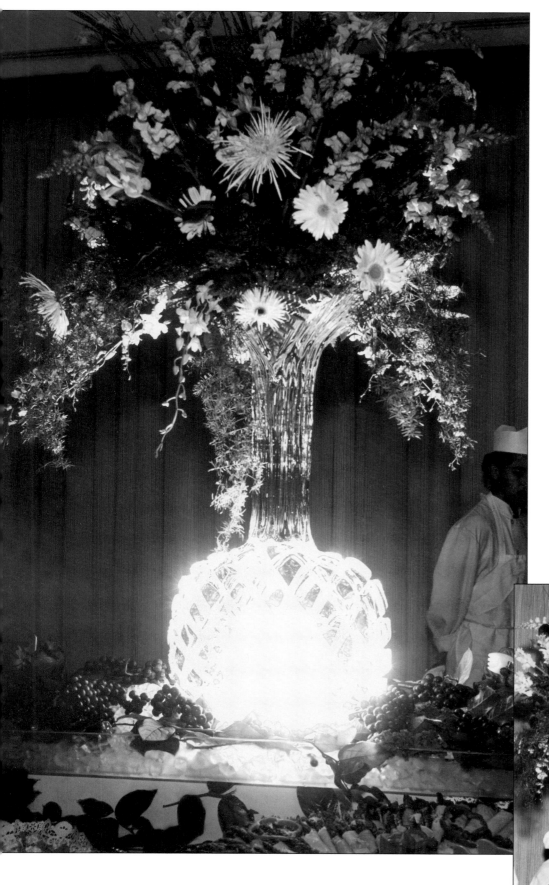
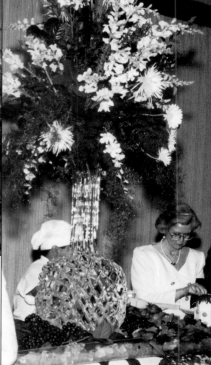

☐ Prop

Remember, there are hundreds of special details that have carefully planned – flowers, centerpieces, details of the bride's dress, ribbons, etc. Both close-up and full-view images are needed. A lot of time and money is spent for these details. Record them!

☐ Photography

I do a lot of twin lighting on these images because twin lighting adds detail to these smaller subjects. Use all the lenses in your tool box for lots of different views. The 120mm lens on the Hasselblad is a great lens for this type of photography because of its close focusing ability.

☐ Psychology

I feel it is very important to ask a lot of questions, listen and take notes when you visit with the bride and groom. Ask probing questions, not just, "How many bridesmaids will there be?" Find out what is in her heart, what her dream is, what her fantasy is.

Here are just a few of the questions I ask to find out what she really wants in her wedding photography.

- What type of wedding will you be having?
- What type of photography would you require?
- What is your vision of the wedding?
- Who will be attending the wedding?
- What do you want your wedding to look like?
- If you could get exactly what you wanted, what would it be?
- Why did you decide to have your wedding at this church?
- What do you envision as the sequence of events
  at the wedding?

"... there are hundreds of special details that have been carefully planned..."

second light at f-8
(used as main light
in this situation)

Quantum Q-Flash   Hasselblad camera
set on automatic f-5.6   80mm lens
set at f-8

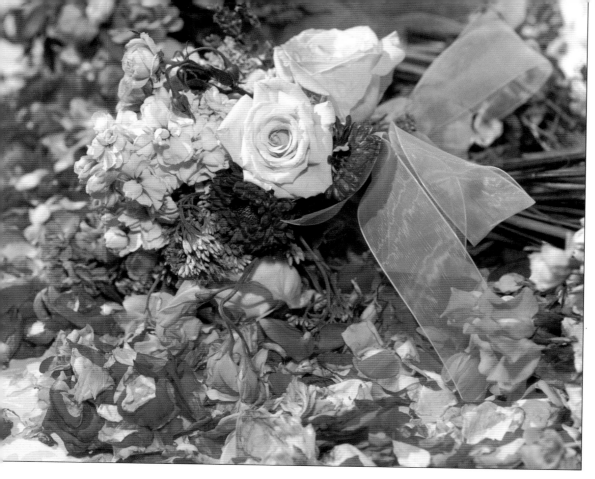

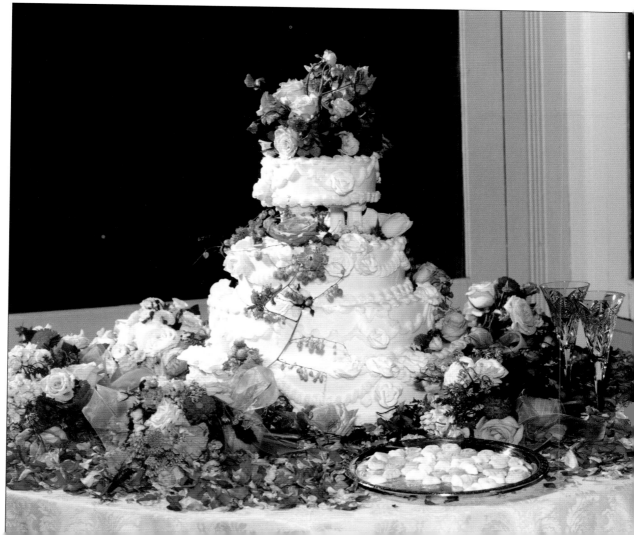

□ Pose

Here we see the same church, but with three different approaches to photographing three different brides. One bride is depicted full face, one in a 2/3 view and one in profile. As you will see below, the lighting was simple, but unique, for each image.

□ Background

The church is the background. As you can see, there are many different ways to utilize one interior space.

□ Photography

In the lower image, one light (the second light) was used for special effects. It is placed low behind the bride. In this image, I turned off the on-camera light to create a backlit effect. I raised the shutter speed to darken the background and emphasize the effect of the light behind the bride. This also makes the stained glass record properly.

To create the top left image, two lights were used. The second light was placed to the right of the camera, and was set one stop brighter than the on-camera light. For a different view, I turned the bride slightly toward the camera and turned her face back toward the camera for a full face view. The second light added texture to the dress and a sense of directionality in the lighting.

The top right image was created using three lights. The on-camera light was used as the fill light, and was set on automatic at f-5.6. The camera was set on f-8. The off-camera light was set on f-8 (manual). The third light was a Morris slave light placed behind the bride. The shutter speed was set to 1/60 second.

□ Psychology

One of the most important things you can learn as a wedding photographer is to work quickly. Pre-plan the posed images you take so you can make the exposures quickly and without a lot of hesitation.

"... three different approaches to photographing three different brides."

third light (for separation)
Morris slave light
on floor behind bride

second light
at f-8 (used as
main light in
this situation)

Hasselblad
camera
50mm lens
set at f-8

Quantum
Q-Flash
set on
automatic f-5.6

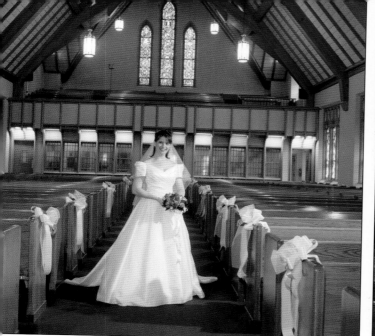
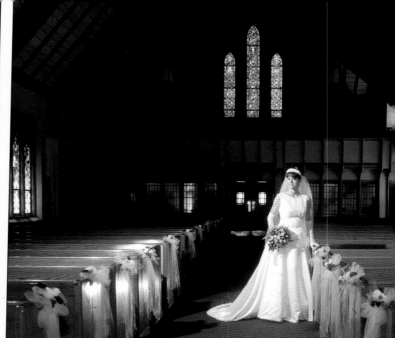
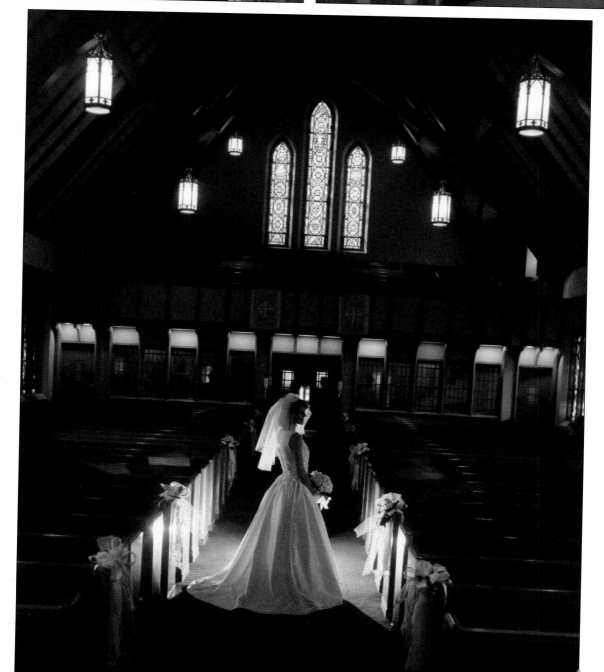

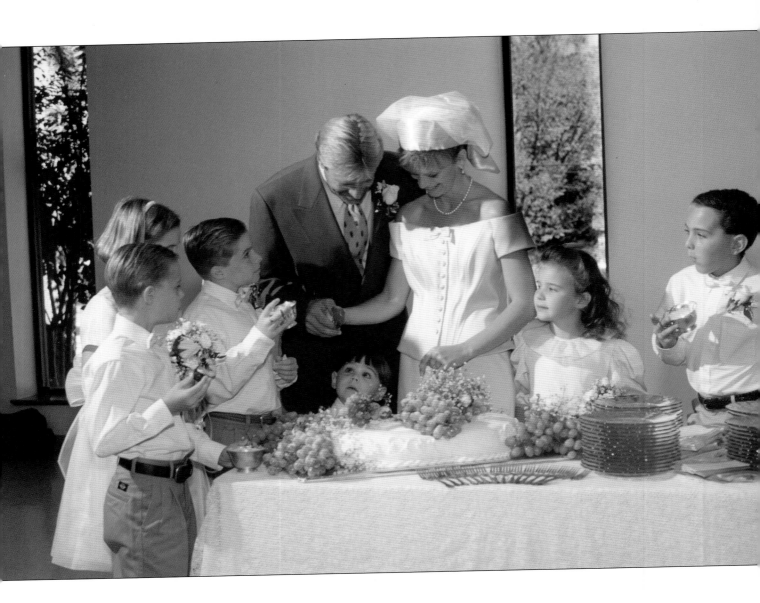

"My favorite part of this fun image is the littlest guy in front of the groom."

☐ **Pose**

This couple each brought three children to the marriage, and they were very inclusive of all the children in the whole wedding. Again, my job was to capture their view of the wedding. This wonderful image captures the "spirit" of their special and unique event. My favorite part of this fun image is the littlest guy in front of the groom. He seems to be saying, "Need some help?"

☐ **Props**

The children are the props in this image. Each one has an expressive look on his or her face. Without the children, it would be just another cake-cutting photograph. I find it very important to look for and capture special moments like this that tell the special story of the wedding. Every wedding has its own personality; you must show that personality in your images.

☐ **Photography**

Look carefully and you can see the twin lighting. It gives direction but does not overpower. The light is up high to keep the shadows from falling on the background and on the children. This is a perfect example of being ready at all times. This special moment only lasted for a second. I got it because I was ready.

☐ **Psychology**

Once more, what do the bride and groom want from you? They want memories – the whole wedding, the way they dreamed it would be! Working with the bride's ideas and style, we custom design a wedding album that tells the story of her special day.

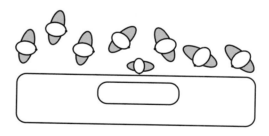

second light at f-8
(used as main light
in this situation)

Quantum Q-Flash Hasselblad camera
set on automatic f-5.6 80mm lens
set at f-8

□ Pose

I positioned the bride and single girls so that I could see them all for the image. I have seen some photographers that break this into two images – one shot "faking" the tossing of the bouquet, the second shot showing the ladies catching it. I choose to make one image of the whole event as it actually happened.

□ Photography

In this twin lighting situation, the second light acted as a second main light. The light on the camera was the main light on the bride and also acted as a fill light for the girls. Because the light is farther away from the girls than it is from the bride, the light is less on them. The inverse square law states that the light fall off is inversely proportional to the distance the light is from the subject. The second light was the main light on the girls, but it also skimmed light on the bride. Without this second light, the single ladies would have been a stop or more darker than the bride. The camera and both lights were set to f-8. The shutter speed had no real effect on the image except to control the background. A slower shutter speed would have recorded more of the background because of the ambient light. To show less of the background, use a faster shutter speed.

□ Psychology

There are several ways to approach shooting any event. I don't pretend to believe that my way is the only way. I am showing a few ways to make some of the hundreds of images made at weddings. In my 26 years of wedding photography, I have done many of these images lots of different ways. The way I approach taking any image is filtered through my past experience with various techniques, the opinions of brides I have worked for, feedback from suppliers I have worked with, lessons from photographers/speakers I have seen and studied with, and my own tastes and opinions. Remember, the bride picked you for your style, so make sure to deliver what she is expecting.

"I choose to make one image of the whole event as it actually happened."

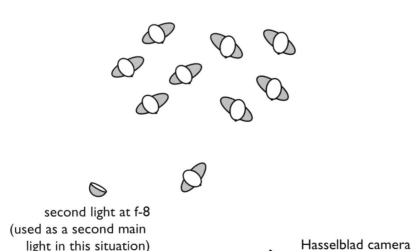

second light at f-8
(used as a second main
light in this situation)

Quantum Q-Flash
set on automatic f-8

Hasselblad camera
50mm lens
set at f-8

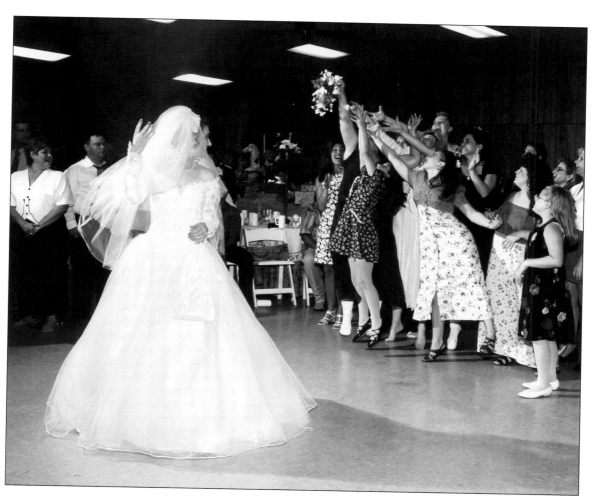

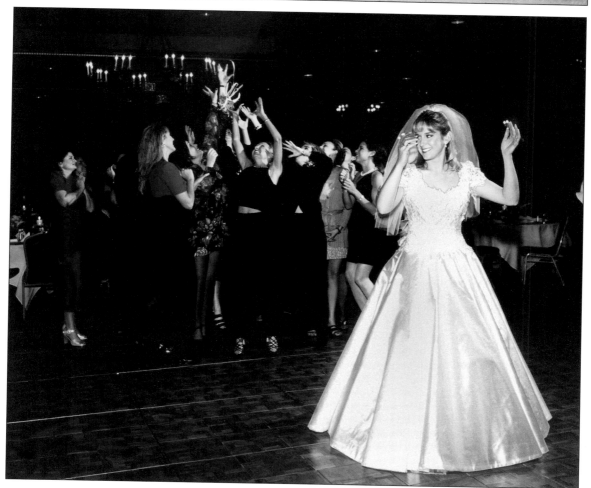

WINDOW LIGHTING

Window light is simple to use, has strong directional qualities and makes beautiful portraits. Using window light is a simple way to add to the variety of your wedding portraits.

□ Pose

I brought the bride and flower girls to this window, and the only posing I did was to place the taller girl on the far right to balance with the bride and to place each of the other girls so that they did not block each other. This image looks good as an 8x10 and as a 10x20 panoramic image in the bride's album.

□ Photography

The lighting used was simple. I just pointed the meter at the camera and exposed the film. The bride's face is not lit, but that's okay, because I was not trying to create a "portrait" but rather a dream-like image. I am told that young girls begin dreaming about their own weddings at about age five – especially if they are a flower girl in a wedding. Here, I tried to show the culmination of the dreams of all the girls in this photograph, including the bride. The image also shows that you can make very nice images with just a small window.

□ Psychology

Photographing children can be fun, if you know the secrets. It can also be demanding. I will admit that it does help to be a "child at heart." In this instance, I simply said, "Doesn't the bride look beautiful?" Every flower girl looked up to the bride. In that moment, I think they began their dream of one day being brides themselves.

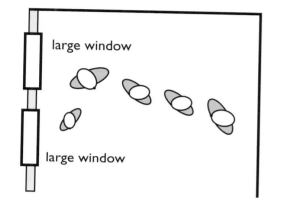

large window

large window

Hasselblad camera
120mm lens

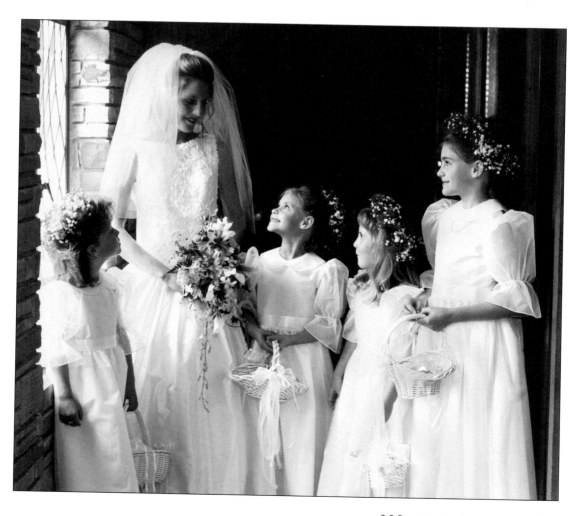

□ Pose

The beautiful young flower girl was standing near the window and the bride walked up, bent over and began to talk to the child. Is it perfect? No. The flower girl could have looked a little more toward the camera or more away from the camera. The way it is, we have a modified 2/3 view of the face. However, I don't care – I like the image. I don't think the pose has to be technically perfect to yield a very nice image. In fact, because I did not over-refine the pose, the image looks even better in my opinion. It is natural, one of my favorite qualities in beautiful images.

□ Props

The props are the flowers, both the bride's and the flower girl's. The flowers tend to stop your eye from leaving the central part of the photograph, the faces and the expressions.

□ Background

The background is a hall at the church with a long row of windows along the side. The windows face north, which is best because no direct sunlight comes through windows that face this direction.

□ Photography

This is why I like window light: it is simple to use; it makes natural looking photographs and it has directional qualities. I used an incident light meter to measure the light for the exposure. I used the dome settings and pointed the dome toward the camera. In the past, I used the flat disk setting on the light meter, that was because the film was not rated at a full ISO 400. The flat disk caused a bit of over-exposure to compensate for the slightly lower rating of the film. However, with the new Portra films by Kodak, the film is fully rated at ISO 400, and I can use the dome meter.

□ Psychology

I simply asked the bride to lean over and visit with the young lady. My goal is that the "posed" photographs either look un-posed or reflect the fun of the day. I believe this image succeeded in both goals.

> "... the bride walked up, bent over and began to talk to the child."

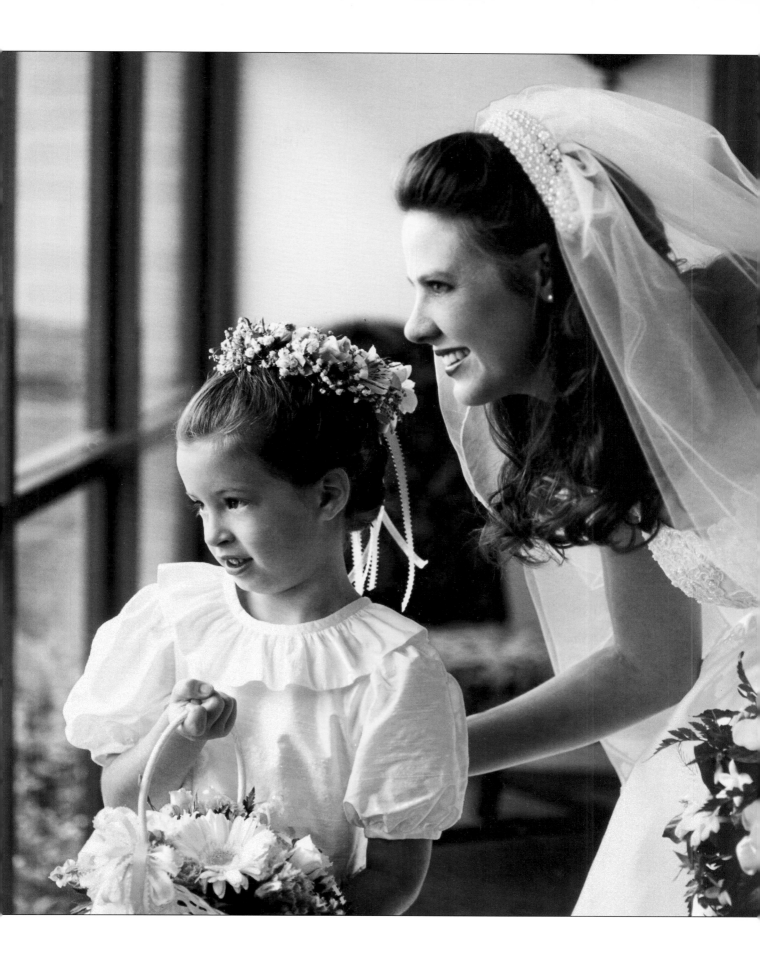

☐ Pose

The pose is simple, yet comfortable and believable. When posing, always start with the feet. Weight should be placed on the back foot, the foot furthest from the camera. Typically, this foot is turned at a 45 degree angle from the camera. Because the weight is on the back foot, the front knee (the groom's left leg in this photograph) usually bends. The point of "putting the weight on the back foot" is to drop the back shoulder. This keeps the body from being straight and stiff. It gives flow to the body and creates a natural stance. If you watch people when they are relaxed and just standing around, most people stand with their weight on one foot.

Another posing guideline with men is to have them tilt their heads slightly toward the side of the lower shoulder. In this image, it is to the groom's right side. This also produces a "C-pose," created with the head and the body. His left hand is in his pants pocket, his right hand extended to rest on the back of the pew. Both of these gestures add to the C shape. This also adds to the appearance of comfort in his demeanor. In this particular image, we showed the groom's full face. "Full face" is defined as showing both sides of the face equally. I usually photograph only three views of the face: full face; 2/3 view and profile.

☐ Background

This Catholic church in Brenham, Texas, is a great place to photograph because of the architecture and large number of windows. I wanted to show the sanctuary as the background. Notice the placement of the groom's head against a plain part of the background. I moved the camera to keep the lines of the background from intersecting with his head. This kept distracting elements from appearing to come out of his head. The camera placement also shows the column, adding strength and balancing with the darkness of the groom's tux.

☐ Photography

Another factor in choosing this composition is the double doors that were to my left. Light through these doors illuminated the groom. Metering the shot was simple. I placed the meter near the groom's face, pointed directly at the camera. By pointing the meter at the camera, you "average" or take into consideration both the main light (coming from the door) and the fill light (overall illumination in the room). Due to the architecture of the building, the overall luminescence provided by the stained glass windows and the indirect light coming through the open doors created a very nice balance of illumination between the subject and the background.

☐ Psychology

You have to earn the respect of the people you photograph. This is especially important at a wedding. You need the cooperation of the participants in order to do your job well. If the people you will be photographing respect you and your task, they will be more cooperative and make your assignment easier. Treat them with respect and don't be bossy. Take control, but in a nice way.

"The pose is simple, yet comfortable and believable."

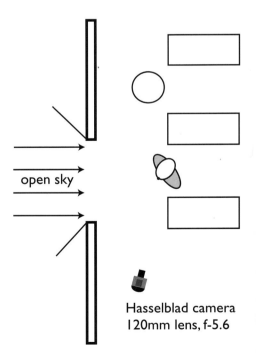

open sky

Hasselblad camera
120mm lens, f-5.6

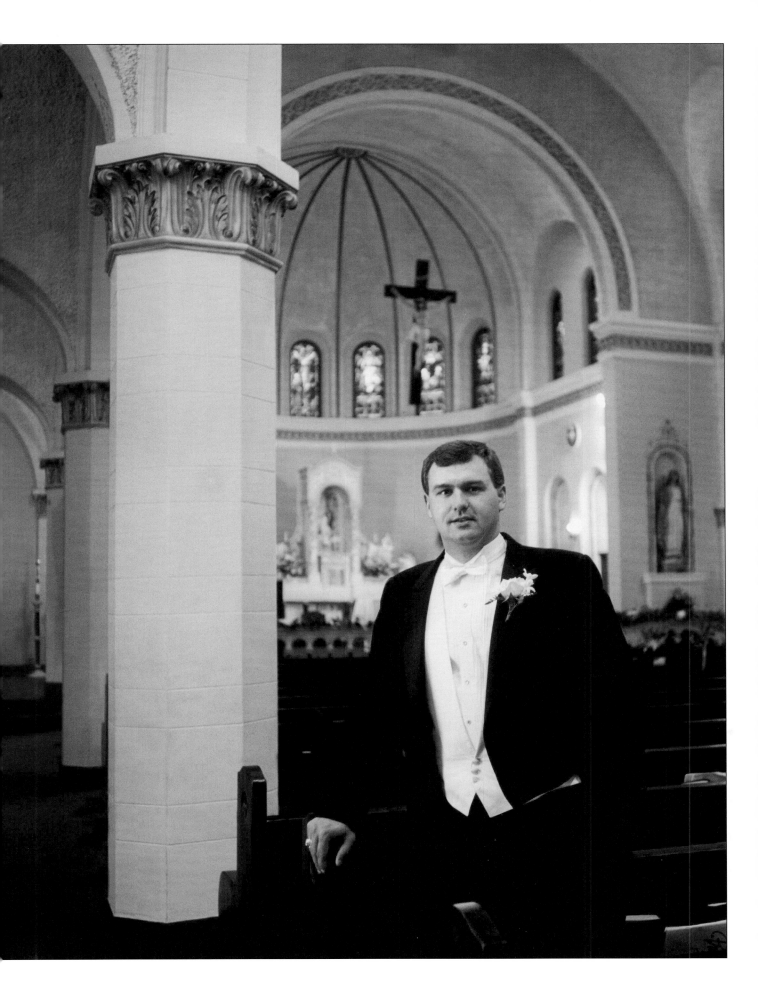

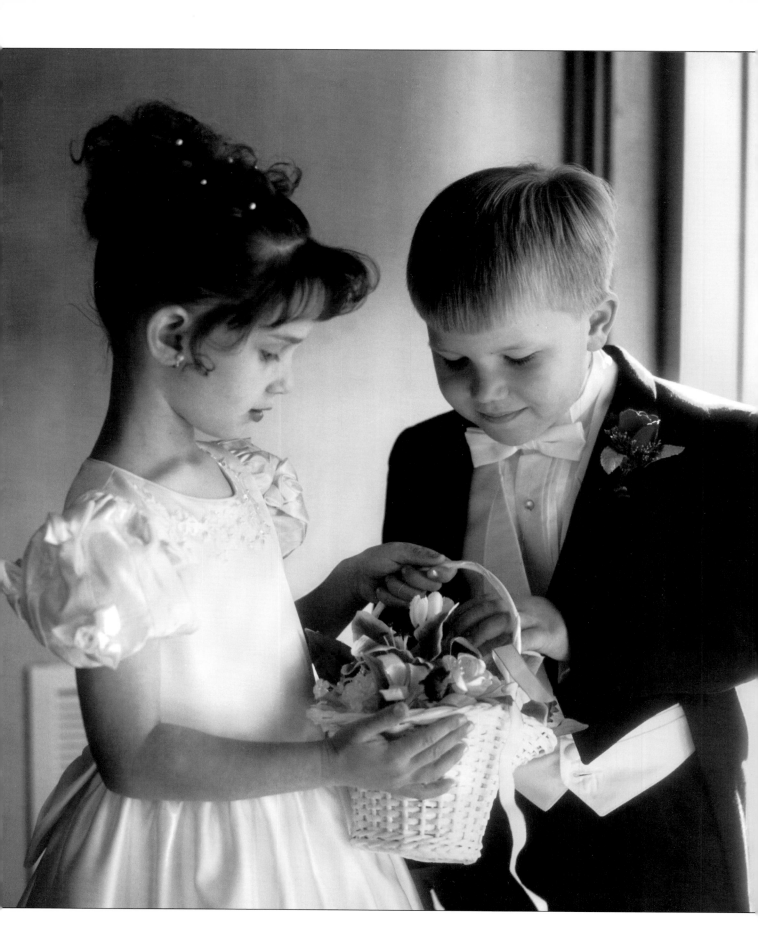

"You can use children's natural curiosity to your advantage."

□ **Pose**

You can use children's natural curiosity to your advantage. "What's in her basket? Is there a surprise in there?" I ask. This will let your subjects forget about you and the camera and concentrate on "looking for the surprise." I had placed the young lady and the camera so that I would get a beautiful profile of her face. The young man has a very nice 2/3 view on his face. This is due to his placement. I feel a photograph with more than one subject is successful when each person is in a pleasing pose and looks good individually as well as together with the other subject or subjects. I think I have accomplished that goal in this image. Place your hand over the girl and you see a very nice portrait of the ring bearer. Conversely, cover the young man and you have a wonderful profile portrait of this precious flower girl.

□ **Props**

The basket is a believable, natural, readily available prop that is certainly part of the story you are responsible for telling. It also works to distract the two from being self-conscious about the photography.

□ **Background**

The background is a door in the small room where the bride is waiting. Several large stained glass windows provided illumination. A phenomena that I don't completely understand is that, even though many different colors of light are coming through the stained glass, it usually provides a fairly "normal" coloration on the people in the photographs. I assume it is because there are usually many colors that add up to the full spectrum of light. Some credit is certainly also due to the great technology of this Kodak film.

□ **Photography**

The boy is lit in the broad light pattern. To determine whether the lighting is broad light or short light, look at the face and draw an imaginary line from top to bottom at the nose. In a 2/3 view of the face, one side of the face is wider (broader) than the other. If the light is coming from and striking the broad side of the face, this is considered broad light. If the light is illuminating the other side, the thinner side, it's considered short lighting.

□ **Psychology**

I have a lot of respect and love for children. They are a large part of the story, and certainly a fun part. Using long lenses is great in photographing children because it gives you a nice working distance from the children, which allows them to be more comfortable.

stained
glass
window

Hasselblad camera
120mm lens
with Quantum flash

□ Pose

Usually a good pose is a comfortable pose. If the person feels comfortable, he will probably look comfortable. Then he is more likely to relax and be himself. When posing people, many times I will first "do the pose." Then I know if it feels comfortable. Next, I suggest they repeat my action. That way I know if it looks good.

□ Background

A window in the balcony of the church provided a quiet, secluded area for a serene portrait of this groom. Light is the lyrics of a photograph, and these are peaceful words.

□ Photography

This image could be a metering nightmare. Do you meter the window, or the shadow of the face? Experience has taught me that if I use an incident meter, place it at the groom's face and point it straight to the camera, it will give me a good exposure. You must know how each film will react to different kinds of light. Consistency is one of the reasons I love and use Kodak film.

□ Psychology

I respond to people on an intuitive basis. It's a talent that comes from years of observing people and an important skill for a wedding photographer. A photograph is a moment in a person's life. Here, I wanted to capture this quiet moment just before the groom was about to take an important step in his life. Instinctively, I felt I had created the image I wanted.

"If the person feels comfortable he will probably look comfortable."

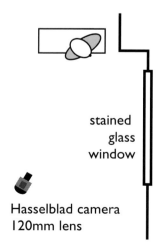

stained
glass
window

Hasselblad camera
120mm lens

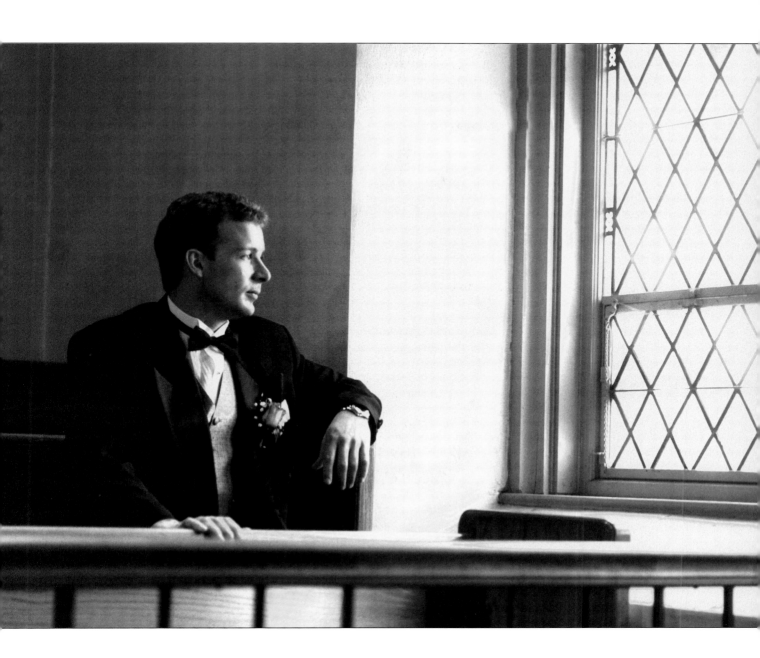

□ Pose

For the photograph with the bride, groom and children, I brought the four subjects to the door and simply asked them to look out the door towards a particular tree. It is important to give your subjects something to look at or everyone will look in a different direction and be distracting in the image. I enjoy the ring bearer's feet – he must have been comfortable with me to pose himself with such a natural mannerism.

□ Background

I guess what I am trying to say with these three images is that if there is an opening for light to come through, you can make a very nice window light portrait. In the image of the bride alone, she is posed by a simple 3'x4' aluminum window. There is a beautiful light on her face, and it shows great detail in her gown.

□ Photography

The position of the face in relationship to the light is very important. In the group portrait, the light is beautiful on the faces; however, if the four had looked at the camera, the relationship of the light to the faces would have changed dramatically and would have produced a very unflattering split light. The contrast of the light would not have changed, but the contrast would have been too great considering the position of the faces in relationship to the light. In the portrait of the little girl and boy, light was coming through a doorway in foyer of the church, which had great brick walls. Add a nice painting and a green plant, and that was all I needed to create a very nice photograph.

□ Psychology

Being a professional photographer means "no excuses." It doesn't matter if it rains or shines, if it is sunny or cloudy, your job is to create beautiful images. In all three of these images, I found a location with soft, indirect light. Even a doorway or a window in an office, if there is light, can become the source of beautiful images.

"It is important to give your subjects something to look at..."

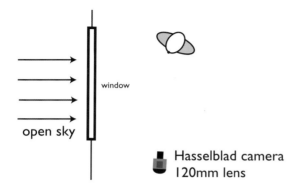

window

open sky

Hasselblad camera
120mm lens

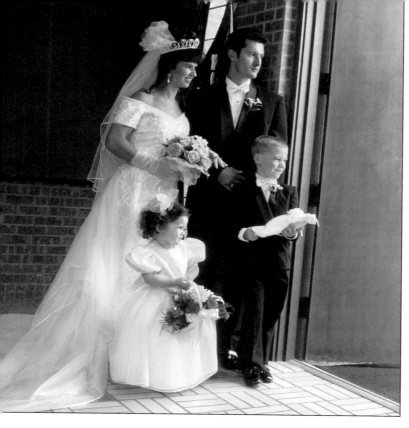

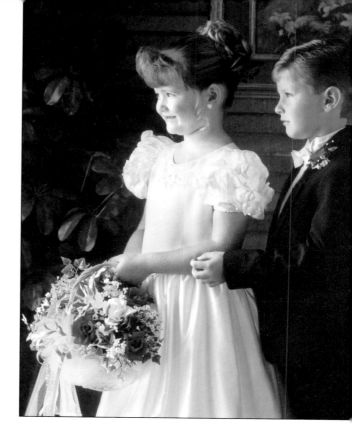

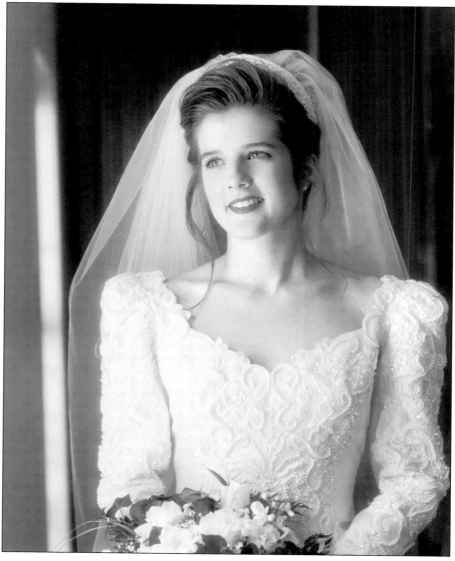

□ Pose

I shot the top image while I was waiting for the bridesmaids to come down to take the lower image. The flower girls were talking to our bride. I love the look of admiration they have for the bride. These tender moments are a special part of the wedding day. While I did pose the photograph on the bottom, the top image just happened naturally.

□ Background

I chose this location mainly for the windows. It was at the end of a wide hallway and had very nice light. The furniture and mirrors break up the plain wall and add depth to the photograph.

□ Photography

I had been photographing the bride by the window when the girls walked up and began the conversation. Thanks to the 250mm lens, I could make the exposures without the young ladies being aware of my presence. After allowing the situation to go on for a few minutes, had the young ladies not naturally taken a nice position for creating these images, I would have coaxed them into better positions. I don't see anything wrong with coaxing people into better poses. My job is to record special moments of the day. This certainly was one. I used the 400 speed film because it allowed me to use a faster shutter speed to stop any action. The exposure was f-5.6 at 1/60. I used a tripod because I did not want to rely on hand holding a 250mm lens at 1/60 of a second.

□ Psychology

One of my goals for a wedding photograph is for the participants to have fun and enjoy even the posed images. I use humor and a nice personality to achieve this. It is important to be respectful to all involved. Granted, you are hired to do a job, which is to make beautiful images. But I don't believe you have the right to be obnoxious, pushy or disagreeable. Lisle Ramsey, a marketing genius in the photographic industry, once told me something that I built my career on. "If people like the photographer, they will like the photography!" I totally believe that. The nicer you are to your clients, their friends and family, the more they will like the photographs. Make the day enjoyable for all, and you will be well rewarded with great referrals!

> "These tender moments are a special part of the wedding day."

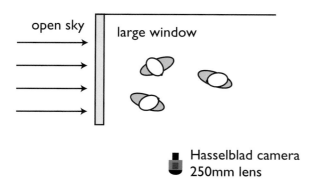

open sky

large window

Hasselblad camera
250mm lens

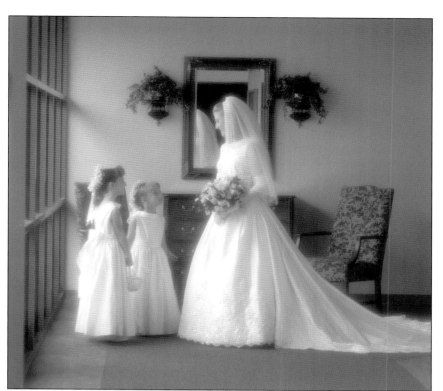

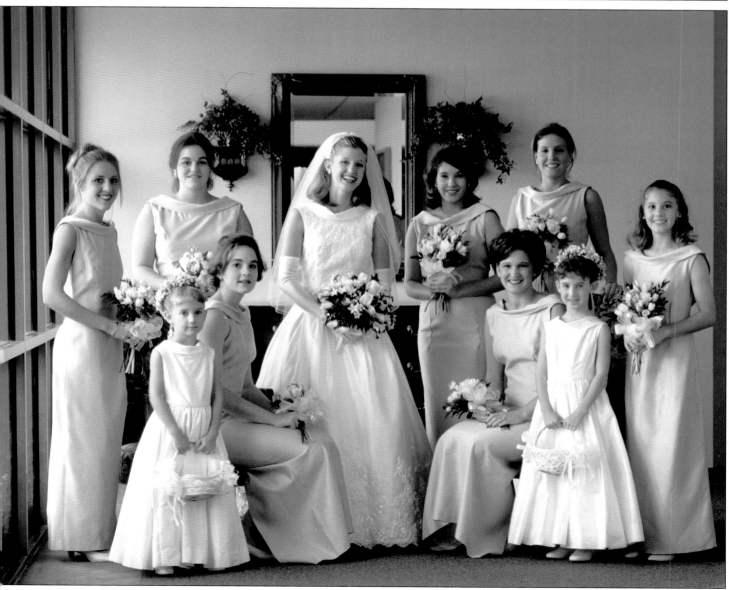

□ **Photography**

All of these images were made with natural light. The metering was the same for each, pointing the dome toward the camera. These details are what make every wedding different and special. Always look for little touches that the bride has planned or included on her special day. The flowers, of course, are always different at every wedding. They are so beautiful and so personal to the bride. At some weddings, special music is also provided. When I look at the photograph of the quartet, I can almost hear the music. I'm sure the bride does, too.

Don't feel that photographs have to have flash added to be good. These have no added light, only window and available light. You can see the direction of light. This adds roundness and dimension to the images.

"Always look for little touches that the bride has planned..."

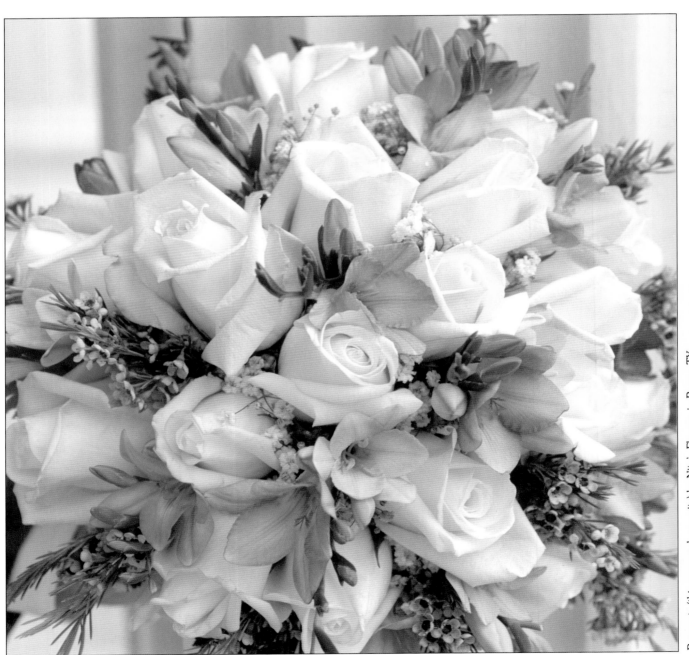

Bouquets (this page and opposite) by Nita's Flowers in Bryan, TX

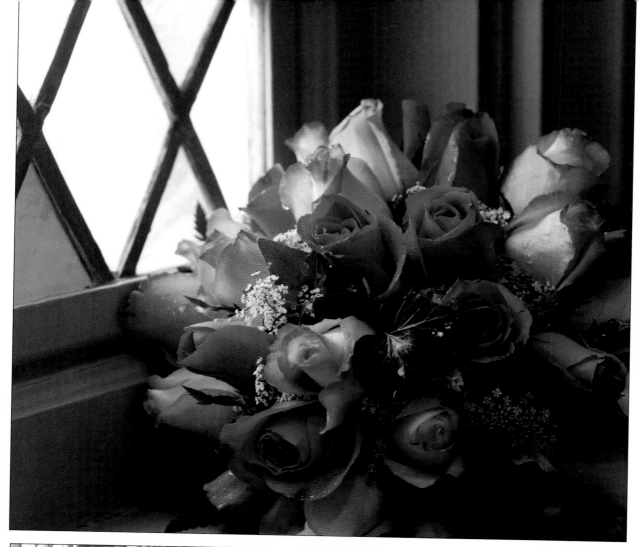

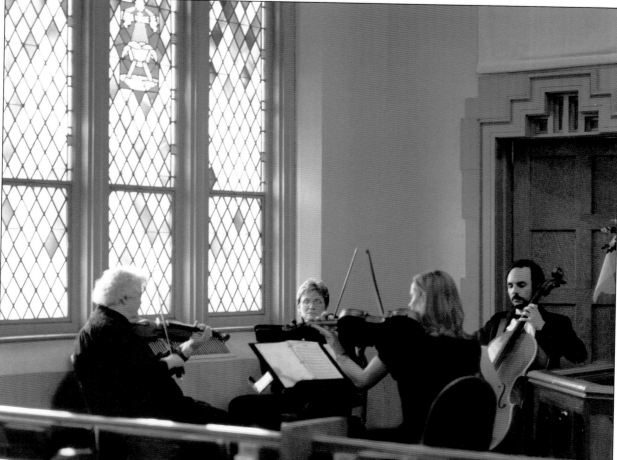

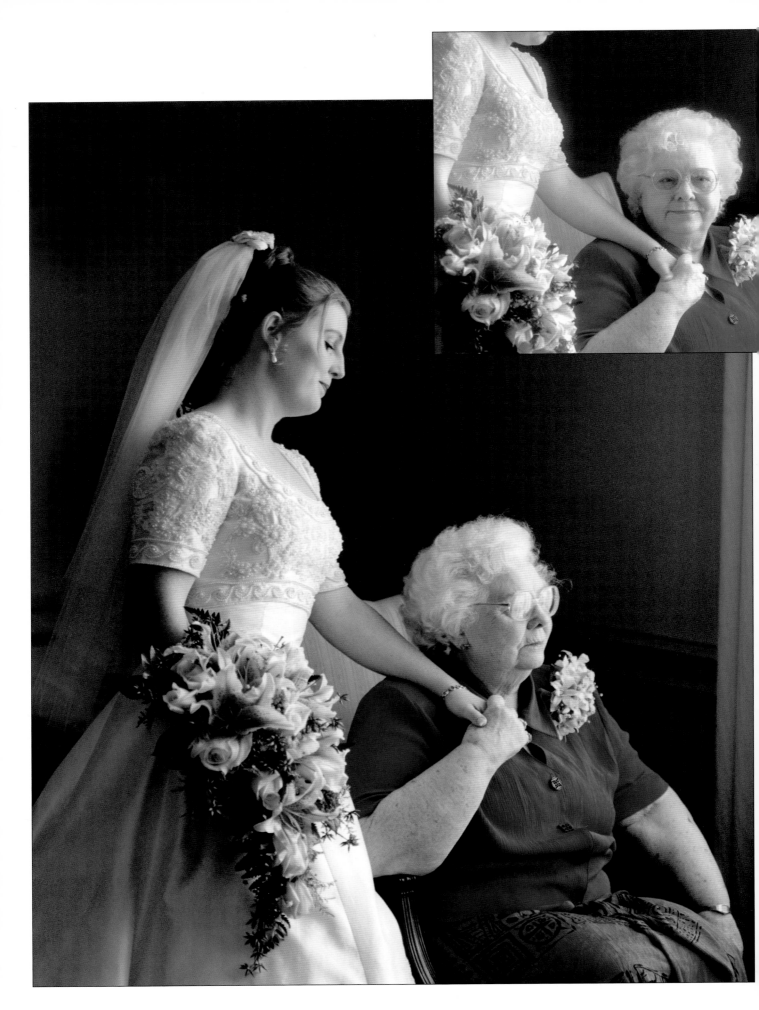

"... she naturally placed her hand on her grandmother's shoulder."

☐ Pose

Again, the pose for this image is very natural. The bride is shown standing, holding the hand of her grandmother and looking out the window. I sat the grandmother in a chair at the back side of the window (furthest from the camera). I brought the bride over, and she naturally placed her hand on her grandmother's shoulder. Then her grandmother simply took her hand. It's simple, innocent and meaningful. Sometimes multiple images can tell a story better than a single photograph. In the close-up image, the face of the bride is not shown; in my opinion, it is not needed. The important part of the image is shown – the love of those two people, especially since you have the other image to set the stage for the second image. I love the way the bride is looking down at her grandmother.

☐ Photography

This image also shows how a simple window and a simple, non-distracting background can make a dramatic photograph. No flash or reflector was needed to create this beautiful portrait.

☐ Psychology

Many older people do not want to have their photograph taken, or at least they say they don't. I just talk real sweet and ask if I can call them grandma. Then I take them by the hand and ask if they will just have a seat over here by the window. I also photograph grandparents alone. It's a great time to get great images of these special people.

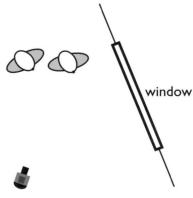

window

Hasselblad camera
120mm lens

☐ Pose

Here we see two images of two people using the same basic pose. I placed the bride and groom next to the window looking at each other and photographed over their shoulders. I love the way this silhouettes the person whose face you cannot see. It seems to frame the photograph and draw attention to the face of the other person. There is something very special about the way brides and grooms look at each other on their wedding day. It is such a loving and longing look. Of course, I then had the two trade places for the other photograph.

☐ Photography

Photographically, this is simple. Nothing was used but a camera, tripod and a light meter. When using an incident light meter, put the meter at the subject and point the meter directly at the camera. A tripod is used on most of my portraits to increase sharpness in the final image. Here, I raised the tripod up over the shoulder of the subject in silhouette. By placing the face against the light part of the background, your eye stays in the important part of the photograph.

☐ Psychology

Since it is very important to show the love and emotion of the relationship, I like to provide some quiet moments for the couple to be alone together. As I spend a few seconds preparing for the image, the pair tend to relax and become more natural, especially if you can get them away from the hustle and bustle of the wedding day. They love these little moments. But remember, do not keep them away from their family and friends too long. This is something you need to develop a feel for. A few minutes is fine; thirty minutes is too long.

> "There is something very special about the way brides and grooms look at each other on their wedding day."

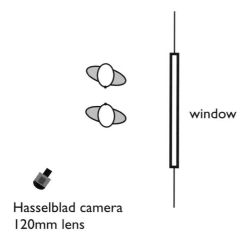

window

Hasselblad camera
120mm lens

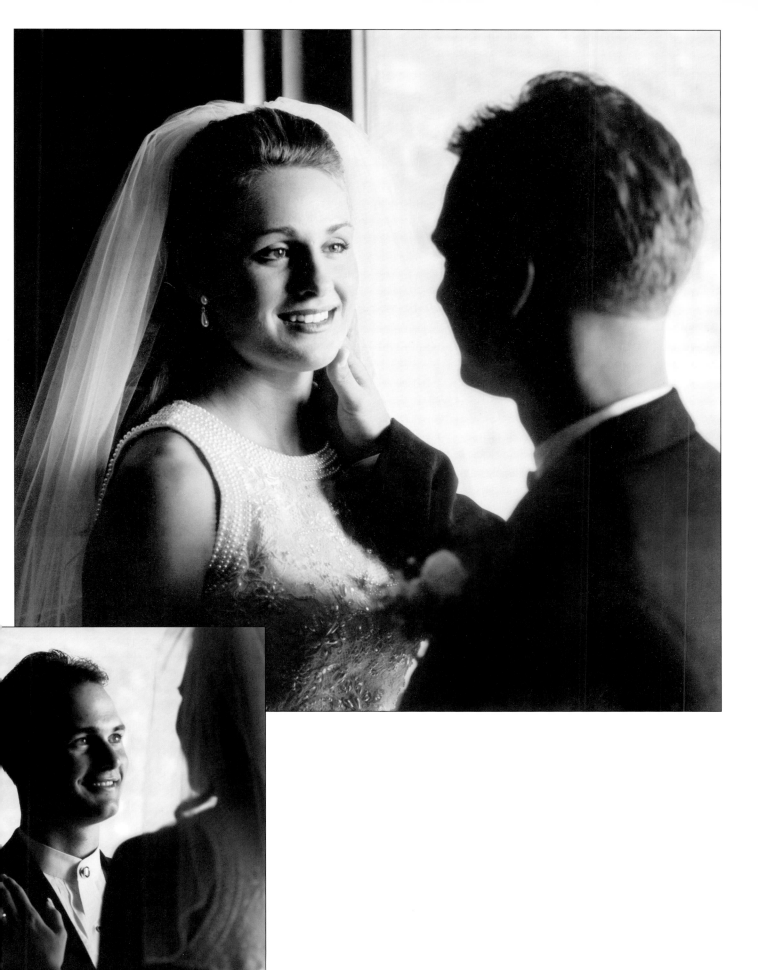

☐ Pose

I began with the bride at the window, creating a profile photograph of her in this position. Then I simply moved the camera closer to the wall. The bride did not change her position, but only raised her face a little. The groom was then brought in beside her. If you place the subject to create a good lighting pattern in a profile view of the face, you can move the camera to photograph the 2/3 view of the face and still have good light on the face. In fact, if you are able to position the camera to photograph the full face, the light will also be good there. The key is to place the person so that the light is at about a 45 degree position from the front of the face.

☐ Background

The window is really the background. I am always amazed when the light source is in the photograph, such as in the image of the bride alone, and yet not blown out. Here, the window still has detail and so does the highlight on the bride.

☐ Photography

Again, I pointed the meter at the camera and made the image. Look at the beautiful light in the eyes of the bride and groom. Also look at the way the light sculpts the beautiful shape of the bride in the profile image. As I teach photographers around the country, I am amazed at how many photographers don't do window light images at weddings, or would have added flash with an image like this. You can make great photographs with window light alone, if you learn to use it properly.

☐ Film

Kodak has developed a new family of films, the Porta Films. They are available in two speeds, both ISO 160 and ISO 400. They also come in two different contrast levels, Natural Color (NC) and Vivid Color (VC). ISO 160 and ISO 400 come in both contrasts. There are several reasons that you should consider using these films for photographing weddings. First, all of these films perfectly match each other in colors. That means you can use any of the films in any combination and put all of the photographs in the same album because the colors will match. Second, these films can handle an incredible range of over- and under-exposure, called exposure latitude. I have run tests and can get very good images with negatives two stops over-exposed to two stops under-exposed. In fact, during one of the tests, the flash did not fire on one exposure, so the only illumination was the small amount of ambient light in the room. The resulting image was *four* stops underexposed. To my total shock, I still got a fairly good image. It was not a great photograph, but if this had been the only image of someone important at a wedding, it would have been acceptable. The way I look at it, using this film is like having a back-up photographer along with you at *every* wedding. Finally, another important reason for using Kodak film is the Promise of Excellence program, through which Kodak guarantees the images against fading. Contact Eastman Kodak for more information on this program.

"The bride did not change her position, but only raised her face a little."

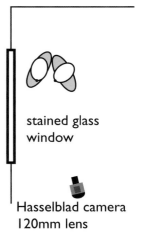

stained glass window

Hasselblad camera
120mm lens

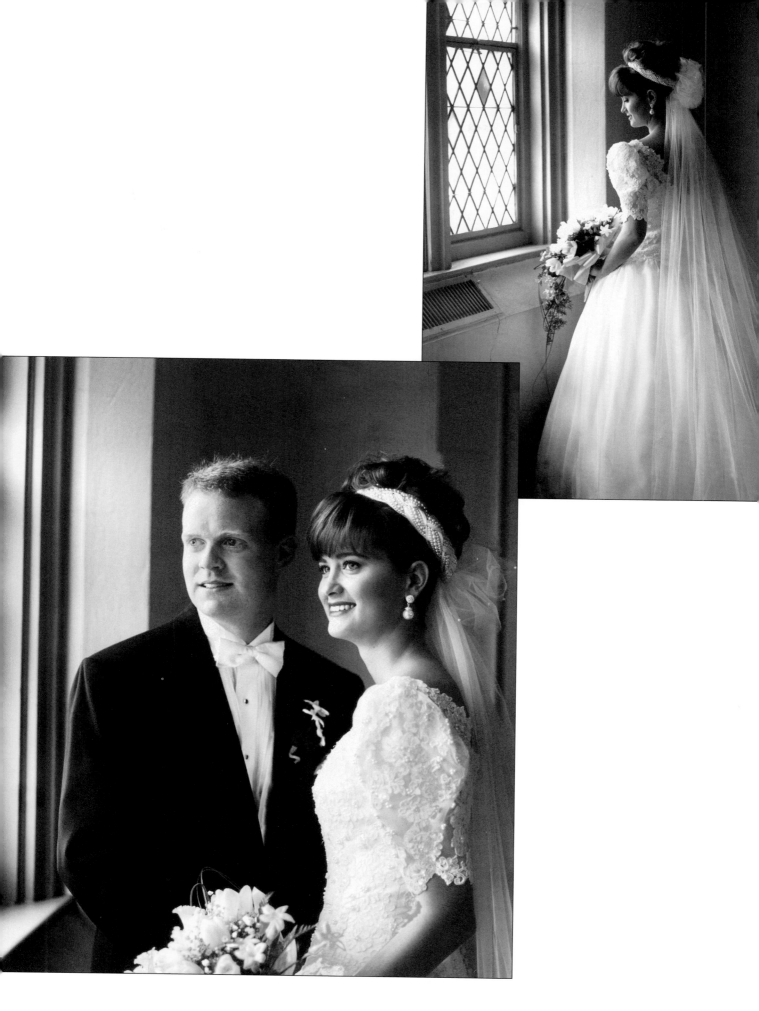

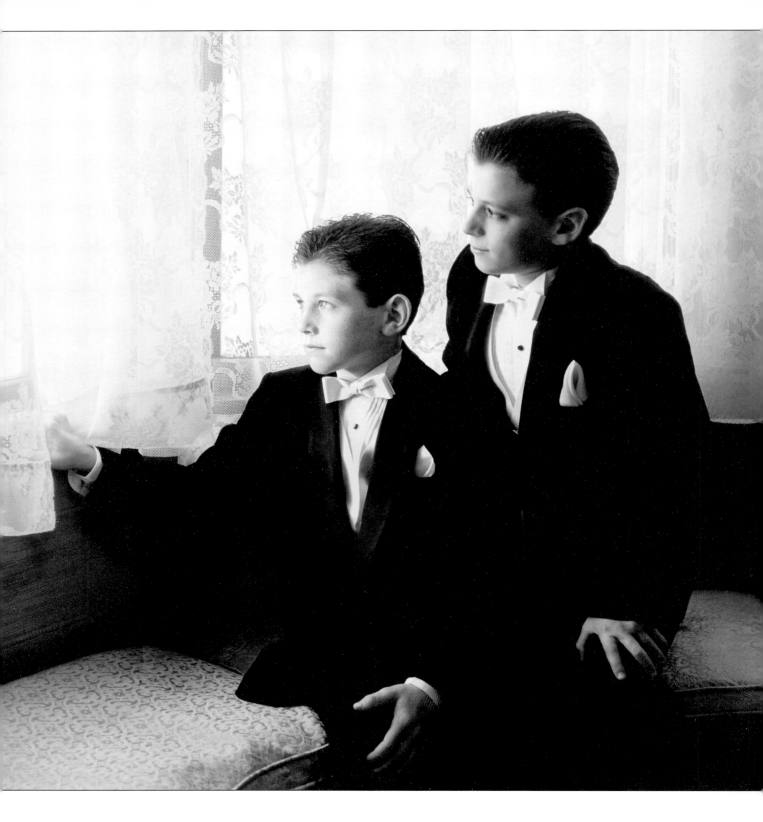

"... if you leave children alone, they will probably pose themselves."

□ Pose

As you can see throughout this book, if you leave children alone, they will probably pose themselves. This pose shows how these two brothers felt about the excitement of the day. Young boys are so cute because of their curiosity. Their mom was getting married this day, and they were in the wedding. In fact, they were a very special part of the wedding, and they took their role very seriously. I wanted this image to show both their curiosity and seriousness.

□ Props

The prop for this portrait is the window. It shows off the location at which the ceremony was taking place. The young men were seated on the bench seat built into the window.

□ Photography

The light coming through the window illuminated the faces of the two boys. I used the 120mm lens on the Hasselblad camera to capture the shot. The medium telephoto lens allowed me to get back from the subjects a little and prevented the distortion that sometimes comes from using a normal or wide-angle lens for close-ups. I placed the faces in the top right hand corner with space in front of them. This gives a comfortable feel to the image.

□ Psychology

When young boys reach this age, they are torn between being boys and being men. Do they goof around or act serious? I find that talking with them like they were adults earns me more cooperation than acting like they were little kids. I try to have respect for all of the people I photograph.

□ Wedding Consultants

Wedding consultants and planners can be a great asset for you at a wedding. You both have a job to do – to make the day special and enjoyable for the bride. I work with two wedding planners on a regular basis (Dorothy Lackey of Weddings, Etc. in Bryan, TX and Margie Young of Events by Room Service in Brenham, TX). Both do a great job for the brides they work with, and take the pressure off me. At weddings without wedding consultants, I sometimes have to make sure things are happening on time.

Both planners have also recommended me for quite a few weddings – and there's nothing better than a personal recommendation from another vendor in the wedding business. Brides trust their experienced opinions and often follow their advice.

Developing a good relationship with the other wedding suppliers in your area will benefit you greatly. I make photographs of the weddings that we work on together and give them copies for their sample albums. Of course, I gold-stamp my name on the front of the photograph and place a label with my studio information on the back. In some instances, I have made complete albums for particular vendors.

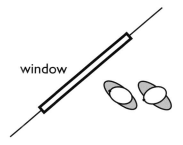

window

Hasselblad camera
120mm lens

AVAILABLE LIGHT

Available light can come from a variety of sources – incandescent light, window light, even candle light, whatever is available. If you learn to use the light you have, no matter what the source, you can create beautiful images.

"I use both black & white and color film for available light."

☐ Film

One of the choices you need to make when using available light is what film to use. I use both black & white and color film for available light images. The black & white films I use are Kodak TriX and TMax 400 speed, and Kodak TMZ 3200 film for 35mm. The latter I rate at ISO 1600 to create a beautiful soft grain pattern.

For color, I use Kodak Porta 400 and Kodak PMZ1000 in medium format size (120 and 220). The 1000 speed is an amazing film. The extra speed allows you to use faster shutter speeds, while still having a very nice grain structure. I have made great images using this film, even in enlargements of 24"x30".

☐ Pose

While photographing a wedding, I did a series of images of the bride getting ready. These were not posed, just captured the way they happened. While doing last minute touch-ups on her make up, I saw this image happening in the mirror. I enjoy images in a mirror if they occur naturally, but think they seem a little silly if posed.

☐ Photography

I love the way the light in the mirror illuminates the bride's face. It adds so much realism to the image. I use wide apertures to isolate the subject and to allow for faster shutter speeds. This is especially helpful if I have to hand-hold the camera.

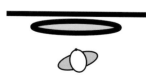

Hasselblad camera
120mm lens

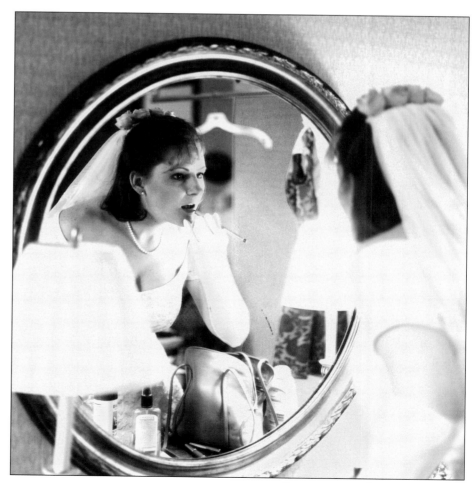

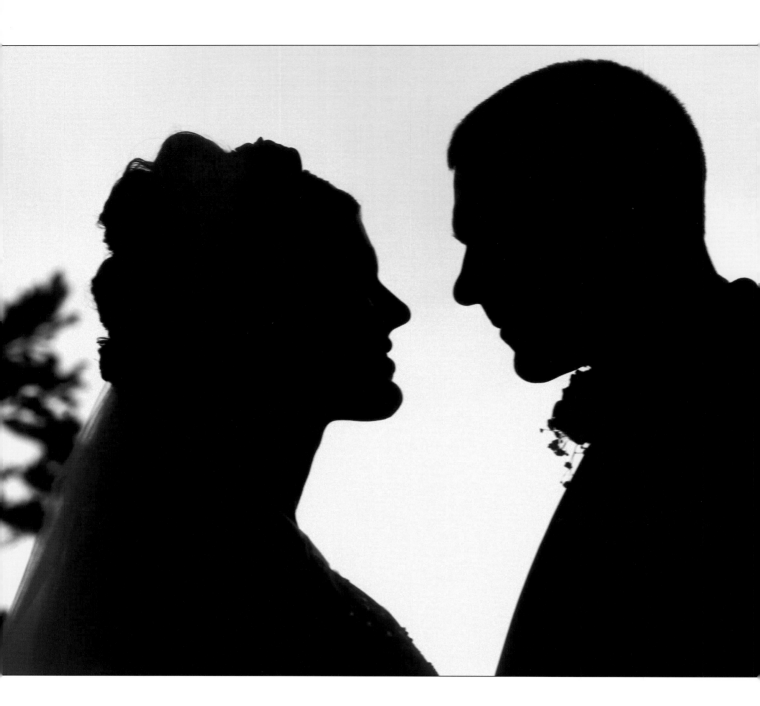

"... they naturally had a great way of looking at each other."

☐ Pose

I brought the couple together to get this silhouetted image. This was the only place that the light was completely blocked off the couple to allow for a clear sky to shine through. But did I have to really pose them? No. I just brought the couple together in the right spot and, as many times happens, they naturally had a great way of looking at each other.

☐ Photography

When doing silhouettes, you need to make sure that the light on the subjects is at least four stops lower than the light on the background. Test the light with your meter. I used the incident setting on the Sekonic L-508 to measure the light on the couple and the spot meter setting to measure the sky. But what if you don't have a spot meter? The Basic Daylight Exposure rule (or "Sunny 16" rule) for exposure on a bright sunny day is easy to compute and remember. Set the shutter speed for the number closest to the ISO of the film (ISO 160 film = 1/125 second, ISO 400 film = 1/500 second, etc.). The correct f-stop will then be f-16. Of course, you can also use another comparable combination shutter speed and f-stop to achieve the same results. For example:

- ISO 160, shutter speed 1/125 at f-16
- ISO 160, shutter speed 1/250 at f-11
- ISO 160, shutter speed 1/500 at f-8
- ISO 160, shutter speed 1/60 at f-22

All of these are equivalent and will give you the same exposure.

There are also other situations that can be calculated by using the Basic Daylight Exposure and opening or closing the aperture by the listed number of stops.

- Sunlight backlit, exposing for shadows = +2 stops
- Overcast weak sunlight, or haze = +1 stops
- Overcast normal sky to cloudy bright sky = +2 stops
- Overcast with heavy clouds, or in open shade = +3 stops

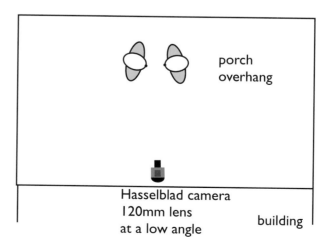

porch overhang

Hasselblad camera
120mm lens
at a low angle

building

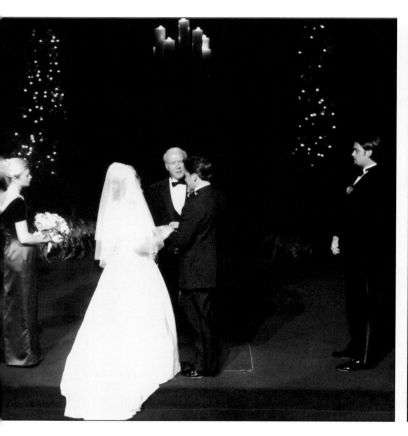
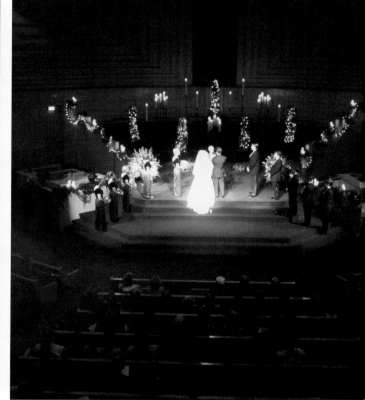

□ **Props**

The props for this image consisted of the decorations in the sanctuary, the flowers and candles. These needed to be recorded and included in the wedding album.

□ **Photography**

I never use a flash during the ceremony. The last flash photograph I make is the one of the bride and her father entering the church, or coming down the aisle. All of the images made during the ceremony are done using available light. I believe that using flash during the wedding would be wrong on two accounts. First, it would be distracting. People would quit watching the wedding and begin giving their attention to you. Second, it is not natural and doesn't show the way things really were. I use Kodak PMZ 1000 ISO for these available light images. The film has a great grain structure and the 1.5 stop increase in exposure (from 400 ISO) is useful in low light situations. Always use a tripod and cable release for these long exposures, which can be as slow as 1/4 second.

"All of the images made during the ceremony are done using available light."

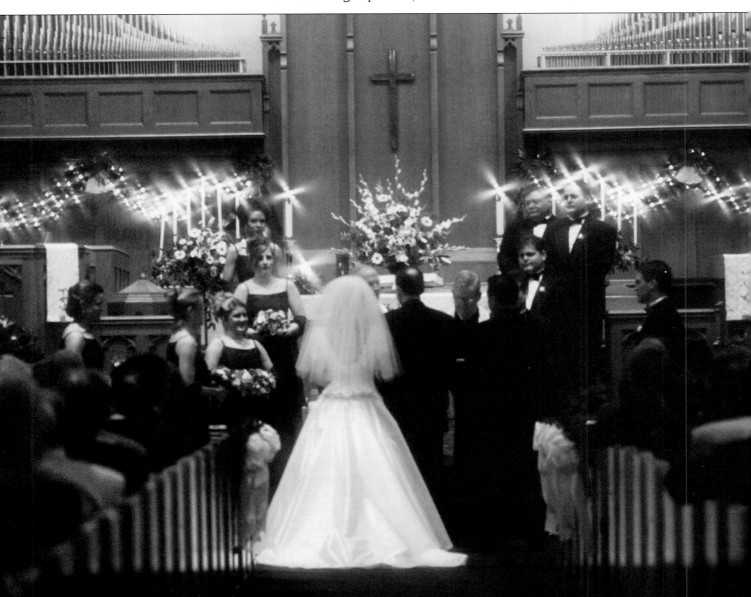

☐ Pose

These moments are part of the real story of the wedding. In the top image on this page, it was raining and this cute image showed what really happened on her day. In the images on the opposite page, I was following the bride and groom from the wedding to the reception, and the driver, a friend, had planned this special moment with the champagne. Had I not been ready and looking for images, I could have missed this special moment. At the wedding, you are on all day. In the lower image on this page, the bride and maid of honor were bustling the dress. One of the loops needed to be expanded, and they couldn't fix it, so the groom was summoned to help. This image was just naturally what was going on. The photograph was made in black & white, perfect for this image because the room was cluttered and the black and white film keeps your attention off the clutter and on the subjects and the action.

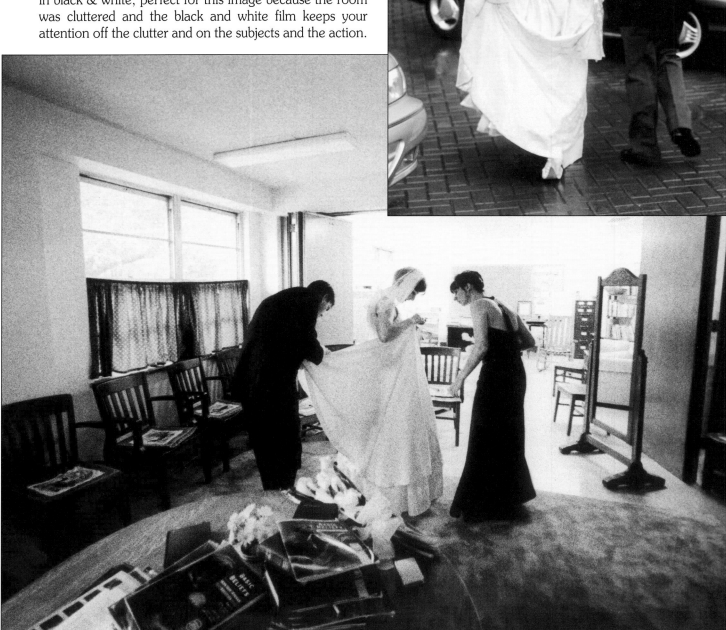

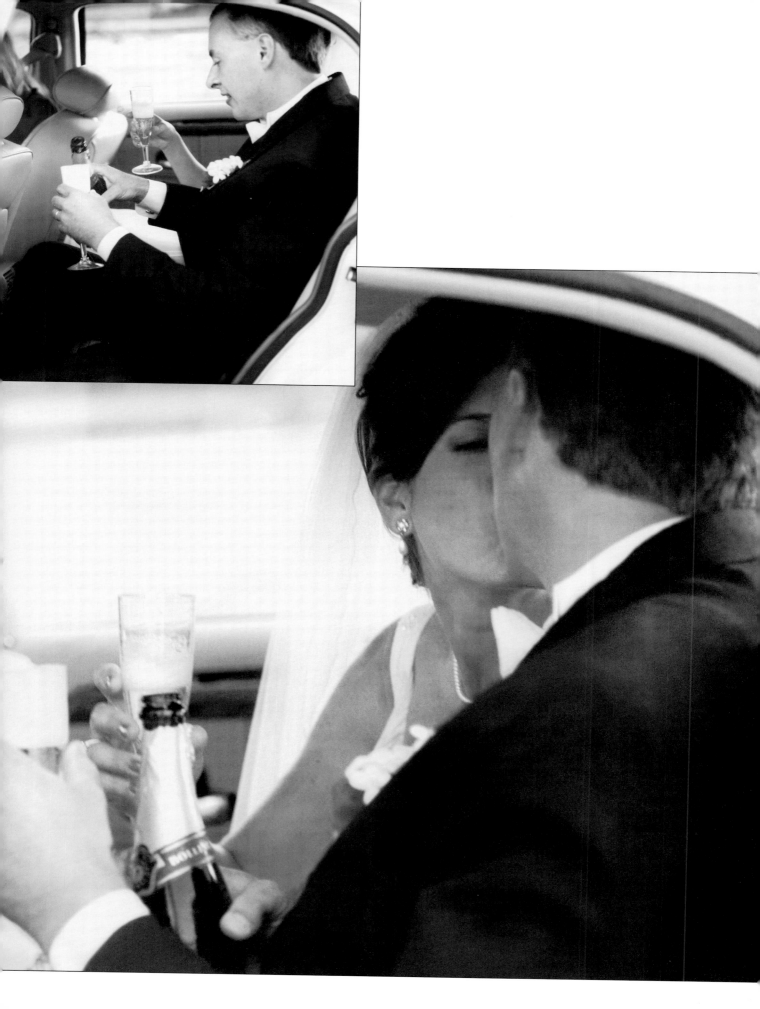

□ Pose

This was a quiet moment when the bride and groom first saw each other. A number of our couples choose to have some private time together before the hustle and bustle of the day begins. This allows them some time alone to spend with the most important person in each other's lives. Brides tell me this is one of the best memories of the day – when her groom, the man she has chosen to spend her life with, sees her for the first time in her gown. This is the first moment that they are alone. I've seen brides almost shaking with nervousness emerge totally calm and relaxed after just a few minutes with the groom. I've also seen grooms with tears in their eyes, emotions I don't believe they would have shown in front of all the guests. This precious moment should be just that, private. I am not in there making photos during this most intimate moment. I do like to capture four or five images of the first encounter, but I shoot from the doorway and use a long lens. Then I close the door and allow them their private time.

This moment, of course, is planned to take place before any guests arrive. Usually it occurs about two hours before the ceremony time. After the bride and groom spend some time together, I return and begin to make images. After this private time, we are able to do any family and special images the bride would like and leave the sanctuary before any guests arrive. Besides spending these romantic moments alone, the couple benefits in other ways from getting started early and taking group and family photos before the ceremony. It means the bride and groom don't have to spend time away from their guests for those images. Also, it means that they can be the first to arrive at the reception instead of the last. In addition, the photography is better because everyone is fresh and looks their best. No one feels rushed. To keep things running smoothly, we develop a schedule that the bride hands out at the rehearsal, telling everyone when to be ready and where to go.

I have to credit the great Monte Zucker for introducing me to this concept almost twenty years ago. Monte is a very fine photographer and teacher. I want to encourage all photographers to continue learning and training to refine their photographic and business skills. I joined the Texas Professional Photographers Association in 1982, and from that point on I can see where my photography has continued to improve and a quick rate. Join your local, state and national photographic associations. Attend the meetings and conventions, get to know fellow photographers in your area and around the country. These friendships and associations will help your business grow and prosper. I also encourage you to enter photographic competitions. These will help you hone your talents so you will produce better images. I have included phone numbers to two of the finest national photographic associations in the United States (Wedding and Portrait Photographers International and Professional Photographers of America) in the suppliers section of this book.

"Brides tell me this is one of the best memories of the day..."

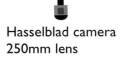

Hasselblad camera
250mm lens

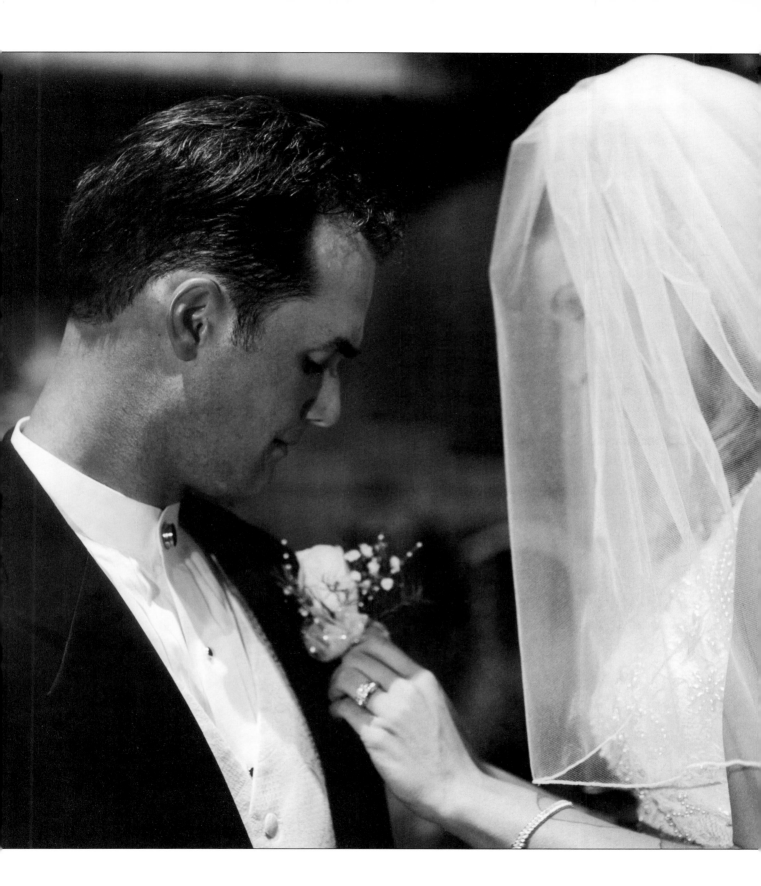

☐ Pose

Brides want you to capture the emotion of the day. Every wedding has its own personality; I try to put this unique flavor into my photographs. Some weddings are elegant, some are casual. Whatever the case, show the joy and happiness of the couple, their family and friends. These moments are not posed, they are found. These moments are not forced, they are captured. Almost anyone can line people up and make posed group photographs. It takes extra effort to seek out the emotional moments, but the reward is certainly worth it.

☐ Photography

All three of these images were made on the Nikon 8008s 35mm camera. The quick auto-focus of this camera makes it ideal for the split-second moments of emotion. I chose the Kodak TMZ3200 film for these images. With only normal room lights, the fast film and the fast lens (80-200mm f-2.8 Nikon) made these images possible.

☐ Psychology

When a couple hires you to photograph their wedding, they are trusting you with one of the most important days in their lives. Months and sometimes years of dreams and planning go into the day. They are spending a lot of money on the event and investing in your photography. You only have one shot, so you should own the finest and most dependable equipment available to you. Keep it in good working order and check it throughout the day. Between each roll of film, I look through the lens to make sure the flash is firing in sync with the lens. This simple habit can save you much grief and even a lawsuit. If you check between each roll and do notice a problem, you can recreate the images taken on that last roll of film. It may be a bit of a hassle, but it's better than losing forever the happenings of the day. Of course, it goes without saying that you should have back-up equipment with you at every wedding or photo assignment. You never know when a sync cord will break, or a lens will malfunction. Like the Boy Scouts always say, "Be prepared."

"... show the joy and happiness of the couple, their family and friends."

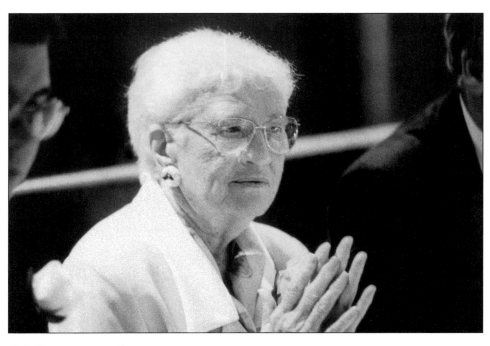

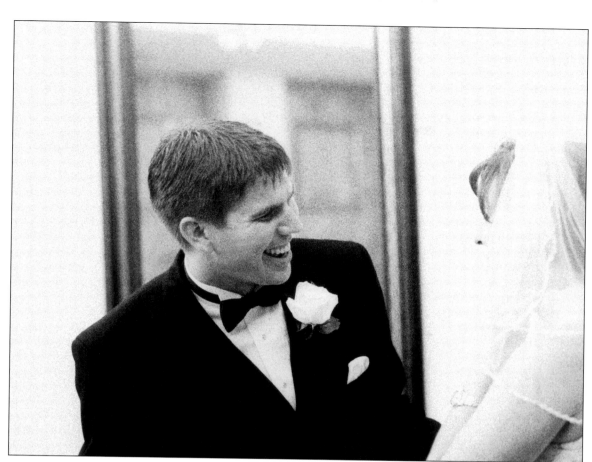

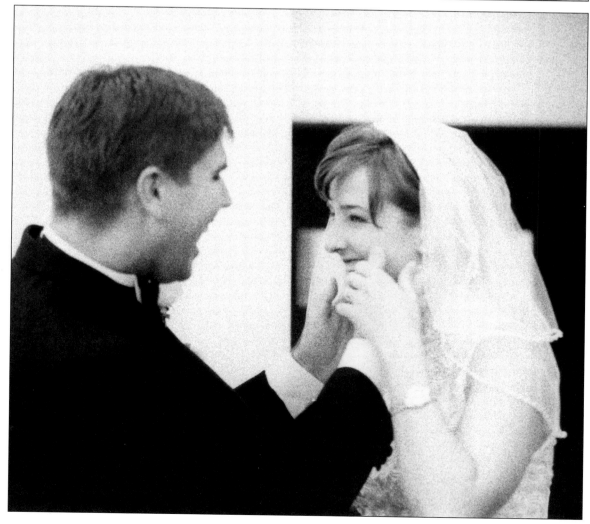

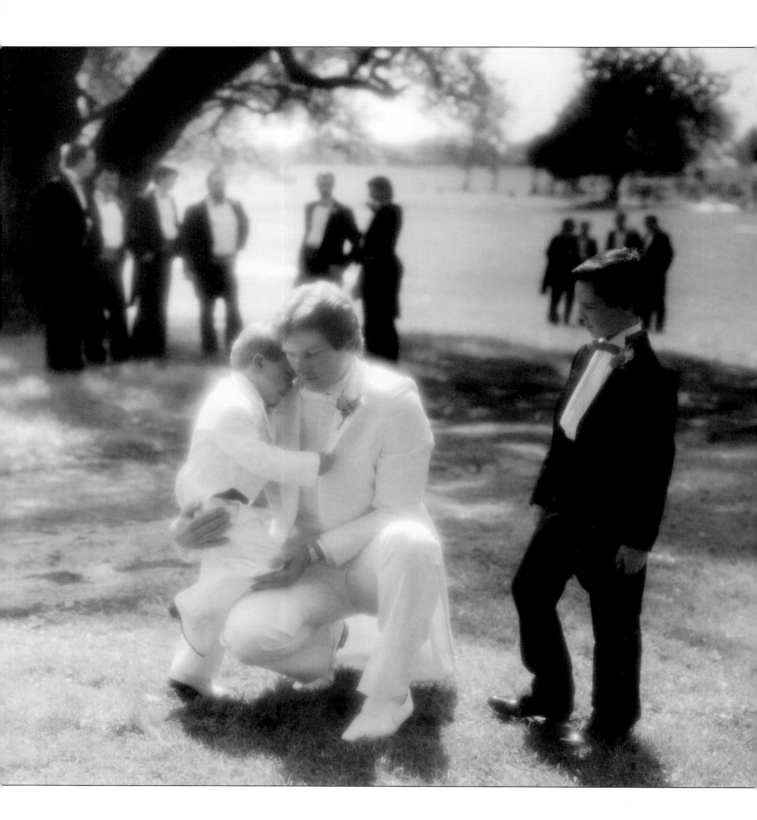

"I was in a very creative mood and wanted to do something different..."

☐ Flash On Camera

There are times when you are working very fast and the lighting conditions require that you use an on-camera flash. Use this tool competently, and your wedding images will look better. Use it poorly, and your photographs will have a very unnatural look.

☐ Pose

There are posed photographs and unposed photographs, but this is a combination of both. I had just spent a week studying with Master Photographer, Jay Stock at the Texas School of Professional Photography. I was in a very creative mood and wanted to do something different with the images of the groom and groomsmen. I had already done a traditional group shot, so I separated the guys into groups and spread them out. The vision I had was to show the way the guys begin to form small groups as old friends and family members separate into more familiar groupings. The groom feels responsible for the little guys and entertains them. As I observed the natural grouping begin to form, I separated the groups a little more to fill in the large open field. Just as I began making the images, the ring bearer began to cry. Many people would have stopped making photographs and waited until the little man regained his composure. But not me – I love the real-life story being played out in front of the lens.

☐ Background

This image was shot in the field behind the church. Look closely and you can see the cemetery that is common in country churches. The old oak trees provided some nice shade to keep too much attention from going to the nearer group of groomsmen, while the sunlight holds your attention on the foreground subjects.

☐ Photography

I usually prefer to photograph outdoors during the last hour of the day, during what I call "sweet light," but that is not when this wedding was taking place. So, as a professional, I feel you must do the very best you can with the situations provided you. When you have hard light (direct sunlight), a soft focus filter is very effective. Here, it added to the tender feeling between the groom and the young man. I used a little fill flash to open up the shadow area on the groom and the two young boys. The film was Kodak VPS. Since the subjects are illuminated by direct sunlight, the "Sunny 16" rule applied (see page 87 for more information on this rule). To create a narrower depth of field (throwing the groomsmen in the background out of focus), I used an equivalent exposure of f-8 at 1/500 second. I added a flash set at two stops under that basic exposure (f-4). This filled in the shadow area and added realism but did not overpower the image.

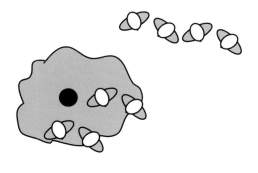

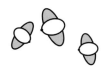

Quantum
Q-Flash
set on
automatic
f-4

Hasselblad
camera
120mm lens,
f-8

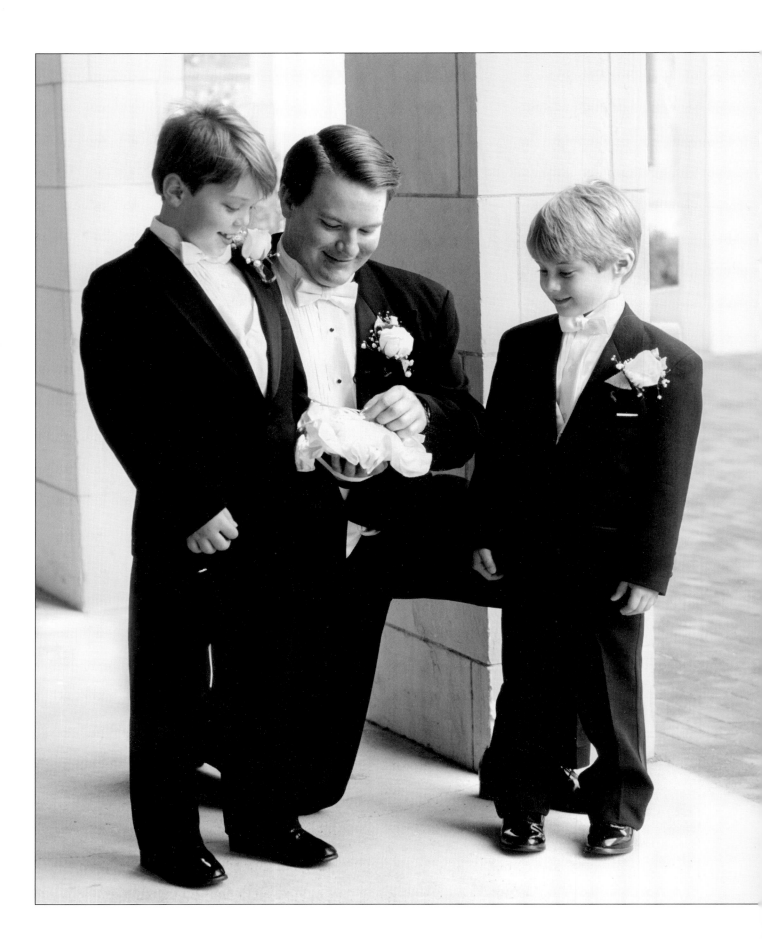

"Place your camera and your subject perpendicular to the length of the porch..."

□ Porch Light

Porch light is very much like window light. Because the roof structure of the porch blocks the light from above, forcing the light to come from one direction and not from the top, it has a directional quality. Because it is typically a large light source, it is a soft light. The starting place for camera and subject placement under a porch is to have the light source, the open sky, at your side, as opposed to behind you or behind the subject. Place your camera and your subject perpendicular to the length of the porch, with your subject's faces generally turned toward the open sky.

□ Pose

I positioned the groom and the two boys so that I would have a triangular composition and so that each face was on a different level. This gave importance to each person. I used the pillow as a center of interest and to give them something to do, and chose to make the images without having the trio look at the camera. It is a much more pleasing image than three guys standing in a row.

□ Props:

The prop is the pillow. By including it in the photograph we accomplished two things. First, we showed off this wedding accessory, and second, we gave our three fellows something to do so they didn't look posed.

□ Photography

Notice the direction of light coming from the right. This is because of the porch. The light is forced to come from the side and not from the top. The building to the left stops the light coming from that direction.

□ Psychology

I feel like I have two options when photographing a wedding. I can record only what happens, typically called photojournalism or candid images. This works with very animated people, but not everyone and every wedding is loose and comfortable. Some people are nervous and a little stiff – especially before the wedding starts. My second option is to "encourage" things to happen. I can get the ball rolling, so to speak, by creating scenarios and letting people react to the situation. In this way, I am able to get natural expressions and actions that would not have naturally happened. I find this is better than having people just line up to "take pictures!"

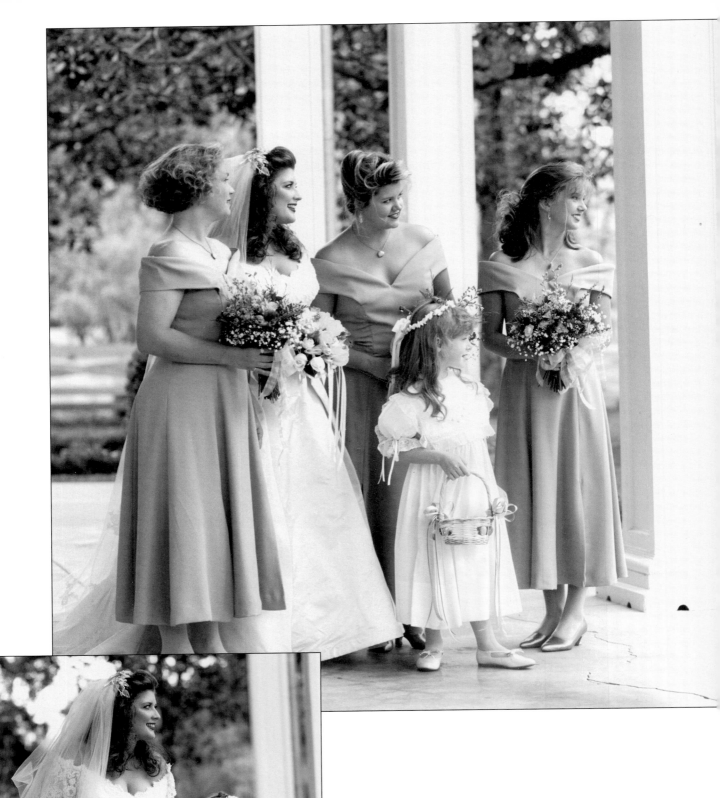

"I get the girls in position, then tend to leave them alone and take a few images."

□ Pose

This is another example of creating wonderful portraits simply by putting people in a place that has good light (here, a porch). Place them in good positions and then let them react naturally. To create an image like the one of the bride with the bridesmaids and flower girl, I get the girls in position, then tend to leave them alone and take a few images. As I was beginning to shoot for this photograph, someone started to walk up from a distance. Everyone's attention was drawn to the person approaching and away from me. Notice the bridesmaid on the bride's left. I love the realism of her little lean toward the bride to see around the column. I did place the flower girl's feet in that position, giving a nice flow to the image.

When posing brides, I take into consideration the cut of the dress as well as her shape and size. Very tall slender brides are posed in a more flowing pose. With larger brides, or brides with very large dresses, I make some poses hiding some of the dress. This slenderizes the bride and brings your attention to her face and/or the bodice of the dress. I will sometimes bring other people or flowers up to give the illusion of a smaller dress.

Even posed photographs don't have to look posed. My goal is very natural looking photographs. At some weddings, almost no posing is required. At other events, people seem more stiff and uncomfortable. My job is to make them feel relaxed, or pose them so they look great.

□ Photography

The 250mm lens, used wide open at f-5.6, made the distracting background go out of focus. Notice the bright sky in the upper part of the image. That area would have been very distracting with a smaller focal length lens. The spots would have appeared sharper and more distinct.

Look for the story behind the story. Some of my best images come right after the planned photograph. I will make an exposure of an event at a wedding, but instead of putting the camera down, I continue to watch for natural reactions and emotions. These candid moments show the personalities of the people and the wedding.

☐ **Pose**

This is a similar image to the one on the preceding page. However, it has a totally different look because of the different location and the time of day. Both are nice photographs, have good direction of light and portray the ladies in pleasing poses. I just love the natural feel and unposed look to the images.

☐ **Album Design**

One of the things that makes our wedding photography service different from many others is that we have the added service of album design for our brides. Instead of delivering a set of "proofs" and making the bride figure out the layout (which images to use, in which size and in what order), we do that for them. In four to five weeks, we deliver a completed wedding story to the bride. We include one of every great image taken at the wedding. The images are in multiple sizes, from 4"x5" to 10"x20" panoramics and every size in between. My wife Barbara carefully puts them in a storytelling order and layout. This way the couple, their friends and their family are immediately able to enjoy the story of the wedding, instead of looking through a scattered bunch of photographs in a proof book. Our brides enjoy this service as much as they enjoy the wedding images. In the past, before we offered this free design service, brides would sometimes have the proof book out for months, sometimes over a year, before they got around to trying to figure out how they wanted the book laid out. Then they would come to me for help in this matter. We started this approach to wedding delivery about twelve years ago with great success.

Recently, a bride whose wedding I had photographed related to me that her sister-in-law was married almost one year before, and her album (created by another photographer) was delivered the same week as my bride received her album. To me this is terrible. Designing the album saves us and the bride a lot of time. It also saves us money in finishing costs – savings which we can pass on to our brides by providing more images at a lower cost. This is one of those "everybody wins" situations. The bride wins because she can enjoy her album sooner. Everyone who sees the album wins because they get to see the photographs in a logical, storytelling form. We win because our images look better in the album than they would in a proof book. One of the biggest reasons we switched was because we found that more people see the bride's photographs in the first month that she has them than in the rest of the first year, because as soon as she gets the photos, she shows everyone!

"This way the couple, their friends and their family are immediately able to enjoy the story of the wedding..."

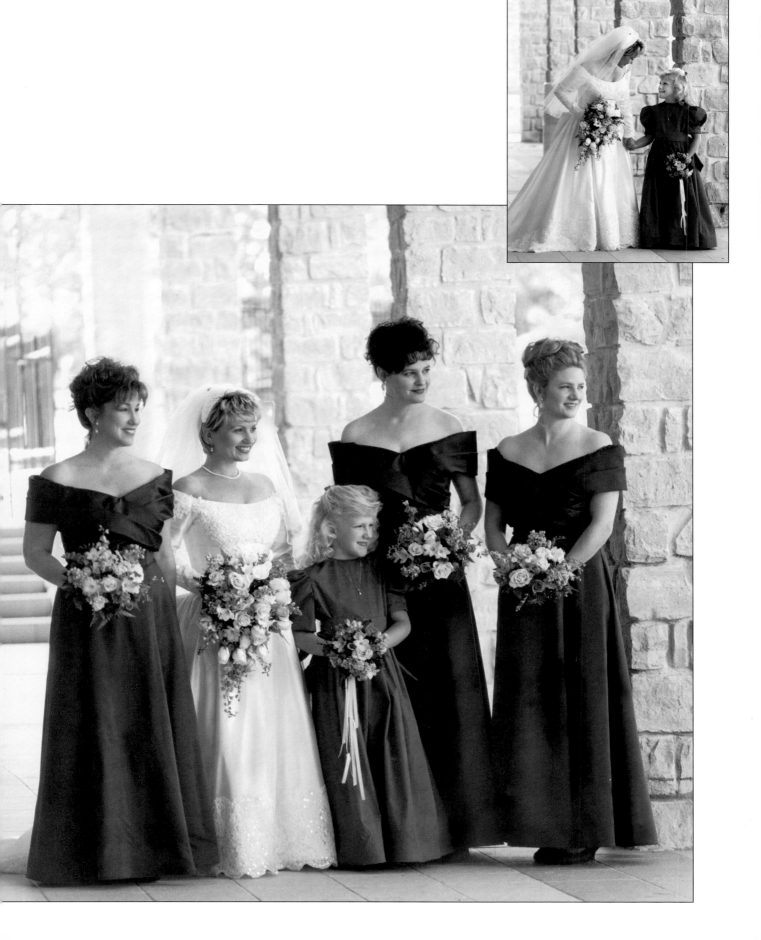

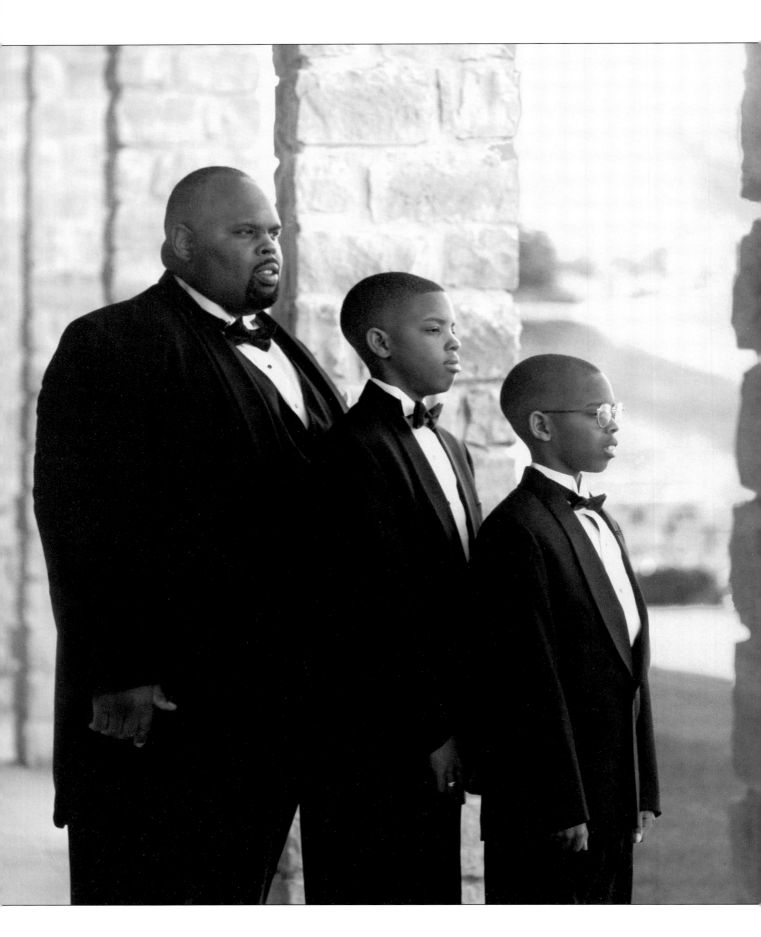

☐ Pose

I chose to photograph this trio of men all in the same pose. This added strength to the image. The pose also mirrors the strong columns in the background. Having all three looking in the same direction gives a sense of purpose to the image.

☐ Photography

One of the keys to great natural light photography is the time of day that the photograph is made. In my opinion, the best time of day to photograph outdoors is about thirty minutes before sunset to about thirty minutes after sunset. The light is softer, has less contrast and provides the beautiful quality of light I require for my images. This image was made a little before the perfect time, so I used the large porch that faced north, to provide the direction of light and block the harder light you see in the background.

Finding the light is one of the first steps in successful natural light photography. Find a good, clean source of light or open sky with light that is fairly broad and close to the horizon. I like to work in open shade in the late afternoon. To select the right spot, stand where the subject will stand and look toward the camera. You should see a fairly large area of open sky on one side. If that patch of open sky is directly behind the camera, the light will seem flat, creating little roundness on the subject's face. You also don't want the light to come from above, since this will cause shadows on the eyes. Think of the open sky as a big window, and look for light that has strong directional qualities (like window light). Remember that a porch will work well as a light modifier to cause the light to fall on the subject from one direction.

Look at the face of your subject and examine the way the light shapes it. Strive for light that gently wraps around, illuminating each feature and lighting one side of the face while just touching the other side.

"Finding the light is the first step in successful natural light photography."

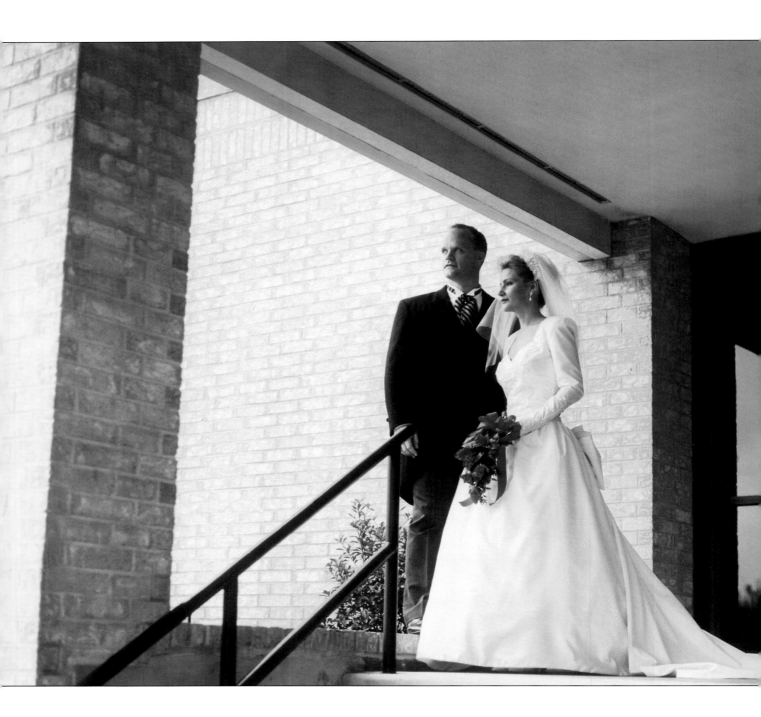

☐ Pose

The pose is quite simple, a profile of the bride and 2/3 view of the groom. Both the bride and groom placed their weight on their inside foot. This dropped the shoulders next to each other, adding to the feeling of closeness and togetherness of the couple.

☐ Background

The background design is one of the elements that adds interest to the image. The lines of the overhang and the railing lead your eye to the couple and add to the triangular composition of the image.

☐ Photography

One of the elements of good photography is direction of light. Here, the main light came from the open sky to the right of the groom. This placed strong directional light on both people. Directional light also gives dimension to photographs. Here, notice how it emphasizes the detail in the bride's gown.

☐ Psychology

Brides want to feel special. Her wedding day is, of course, a very important event in her life. Anything I can do to make a bride feel like Cinderella adds to her enjoyment of her wedding. This means I don't take her away from her guests any more than absolutely necessary. I photograph her in the most pleasing, flattering manner. I do everything in my power to make her feel and look beautiful.

☐ Two Photographers

One of the things that makes our coverage of a bride's wedding so unique is the fact that Barbara, my wife, and I photograph together at the wedding. I photograph in color, usually, while Barbara concentrates on black & white images. I do the portraits and group photographs and the other details and special moments that are to be in color in the album, while Barbara works in a totally documentary or photojournalistic style. Her "storytelling" images are the very things that tell a more intimate version of the wedding. She also helps present the wedding through the eyes of a woman. Women see weddings differently and are more emotionally involved in the photography. Freeing her from doing the "have to" portraiture, allows her to find those special images that tell the rest of the story.

Barbara uses Kodak TMZ 3200 high speed film, fast Nikon lenses and no flash, allowing her to blend in and photograph people as they are. She is in the dressing room as the bride and bridesmaids dress and prepare for the ceremony – an exciting and active part of the day which is often overlooked. Watching and listening to the bride give her inside information on the special touches the bride has worked hard to plan for the day. This helps us direct our photography and personalize the bride's album. Many times a bride will exclaim after viewing her album, "I can't believe you got a photograph of my Mom's handkerchief – it belonged to my favorite grandmother!" We would never have know, had Barbara not been there in the dressing room, paying attention to all those special details.

"This placed strong directional light on both people."

☐ Pose

These are some of my favorite images that show the fun and love that goes on at weddings. There is so much happiness that it is almost impossible not to see the excitement of the day. Still, you have to watch and anticipate the action. This is where the on-camera flash, with its automatic exposure control, can mean the difference between a great image and no image. I use the Quantum Q flash on my Hasselblad camera. This flash is very accurate, lightweight and easy to use. I also keep the camera pre-focused at about ten feet. That way, if I see something about to happen, I can move myself into a position about ten feet away, raise the camera and make the exposure. Sometimes I even "shoot from the hip," not even looking through the camera. Many times I will hold the camera above my head and point the camera down toward the action. The 50mm wide-angle lens on the Hasselblad at f-8 has a great depth of field, so if my focus is off just a little, the lens will still produce an acceptably sharp photograph.

"There is so much happiness that it is almost impossible not to see the excitement of the day."

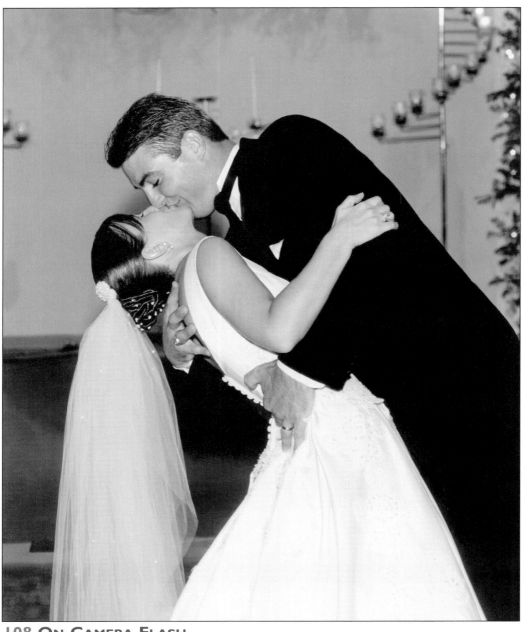

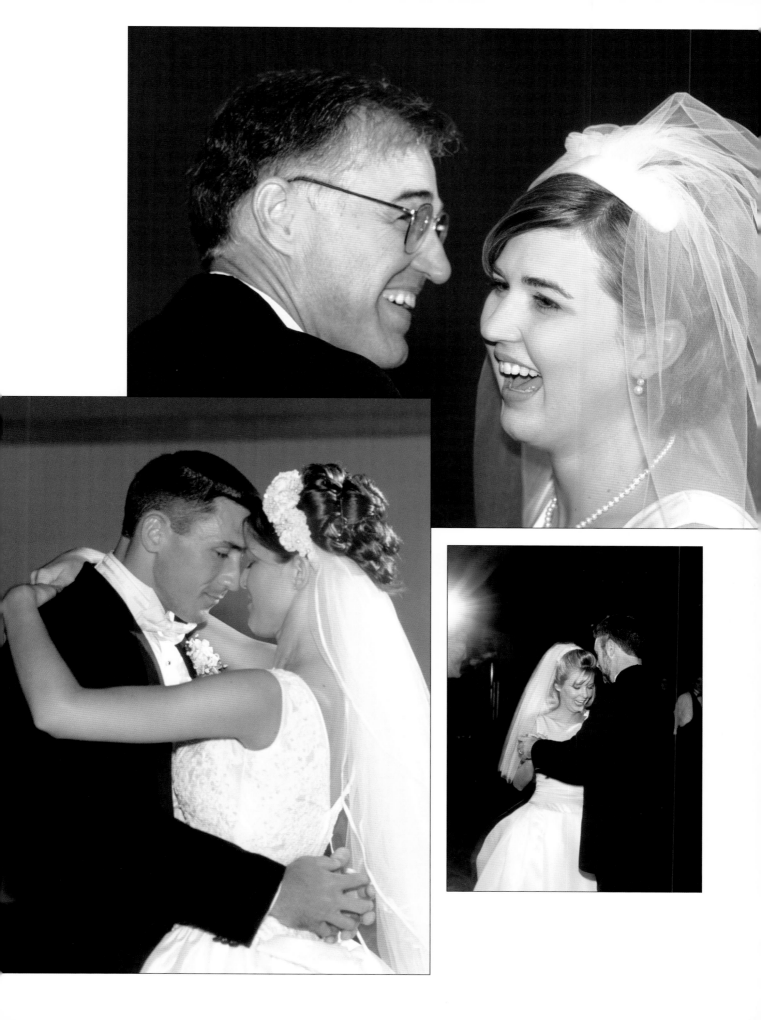

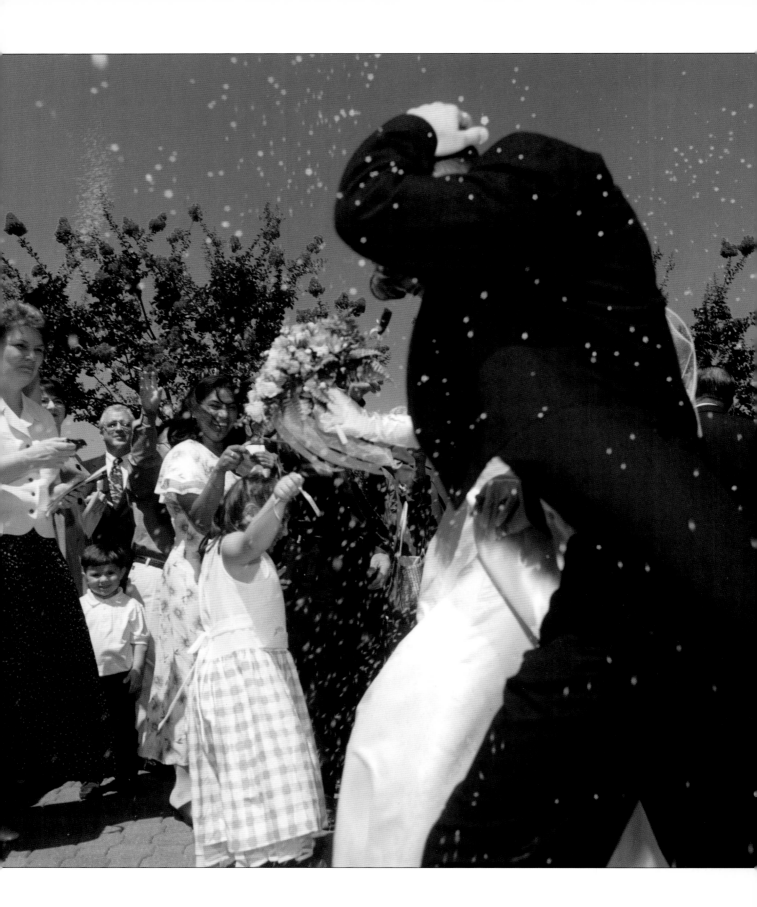

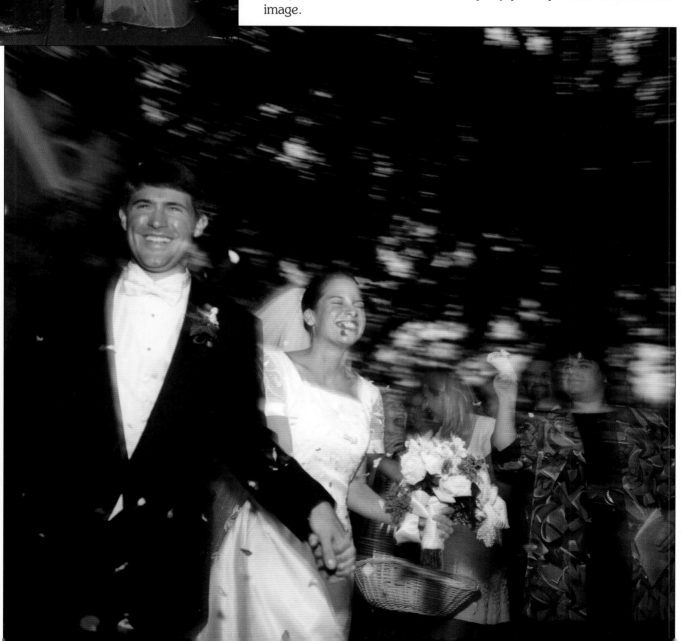

□ Pose

What a great title for these exciting photographs. This is a fun time at the wedding and a great opportunity for you to capture great "Kodak Moments" – moments that show what really happened that day. There is really no posing going on for exit shots, but you do have to position yourself in the proper place to capture the best images.

□ Photography

Again, the on-camera flash saves the day. No elaborate setups were used; the images are the result of being prepared at the proper moment. In the two images on the opposite page, I began shooting as the couple ran down the gauntlet of family and friends. Then I lowered my position to capture a unique angle of the action. The exposure was 1/500 at f-8, and the flash was set at f-8. The camera was pointed up to show the beautiful blue sky behind the couple as they ran by – a truly different way to make this image.

In the photograph below, I used the same technique but with a slow shutter speed to accent the motion. I really enjoy the spontaneous feel of the image.

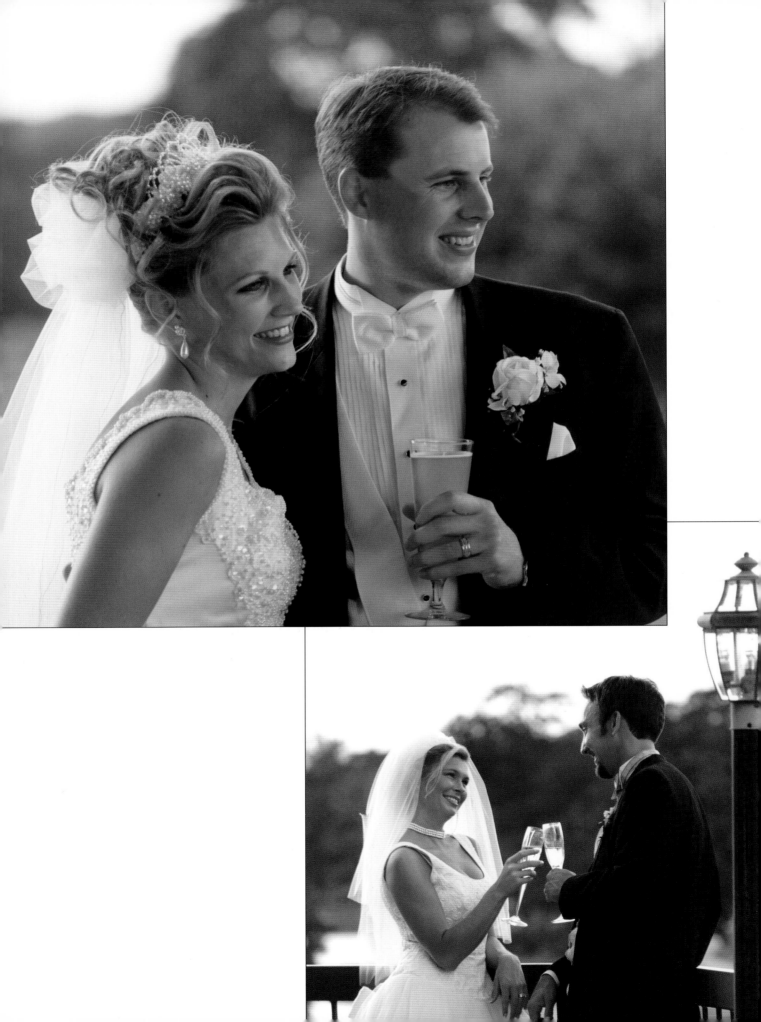

"I love to take couples outside alone at receptions for a few minutes."

☐ **Pose**

These two photographs both follow a similar theme. I love to take couples outside alone at receptions for a few minutes. This gives them a break and gives me an opportunity to get a few great images. I usually take them to a place that has good light and just leave them alone. In most cases, they will react to each other in very natural ways. In both of these images, the couple had their drinks with them. This gave them something to do with their hands and added to the story of the image.

☐ **Photography**

One of the most important elements of good outdoor photography is soft but directional light. This is accomplished most easily by choosing the right time of day. I choose the later afternoon light, the last hour of the day. This light is called "sweet light" and makes the best photographs. Again, I used the 250mm lens to isolate the subjects from the background.

☐ **Psychology**

As I began my career in wedding photography, I noticed that in some wedding albums everything looked the same. The posing was stiff, stale and unimaginative. The lighting was flat (mostly one on-camera flash) and unnatural. The emotions were forced, fake and unbelievable. The storytelling was sporadic, incomplete and unemotional. Something had to change.

I began to seek out photographers to study with who had a different vision of weddings and photography: Monte Zucker, Clay Blackmore, Enoch Hinks, David and Linda Smith, David Ziser, Don Blair, Denis Reggie, Bill Stockwell, Rocky Gunn, Jay Stock, Charles Lewis, Tony Corbell, Ed Pierce, Lisa Murphy, Patsy Hodge, Roy Madearis, Ralph Romaguera, and Gary Allen Strain just to name a few. Each of these great photographers shared with me a little of themselves. They taught me to see differently and helped me develop my own style. In fact, there have been so many photographers who have helped shape my career over the years, that in listing some I run the risk of omitting others. To those, my apologies, and my thanks for their influence.

I highly recommend that you study with photographers whose work you enjoy, and add their visions to your palette as you develop your own personal style.

☐ Pose

Children are some of the most fun subjects to photograph at weddings. They are spontaneous, innocent and full of joy. These littlest participants can add to the overall personality of the wedding album. These two young men took the job of ring bearer very seriously. The older boy was also "assistant photographer." The pose of the older boy is a classic masculine pose, with his weight on his back foot to drop the shoulder and create flow to the image. His head is also tilted slightly to the lower shoulder, and we see a profile view of his face. The younger fellow is leaning into the post, weight on his back foot and his left foot crossed over the right. This shot is a modified profile (not quite perfect but just fine in my opinion).

☐ Marketing

One of the most important parts of your marketing campaign is the paperwork, price lists and brochures. The image you wish to present to clients must match this material. If you want to be an upscale photographer, your promotional materials must look upscale. We have developed an eight-page informational brochure that we send to prospective brides. It includes our philosophy on wedding photography, our accomplishments in the industry, prices and policies, and most importantly a dozen or more of our images. Some are printed in the booklet itself, but in every one we also include actual photographs from other weddings we have photographed.

Each booklet is put together after I have visited on the phone with the bride. I use a phone script (a pre-planned list of questions) to keep me on-track during our conversation and give me a place to note her special wants and needs, her likes and desires. Armed with this information, I create a custom package to send to her. I try to use photographs taken at her church, or her reception area. I include images that reflect the style of photography she says she likes. For example, if children will be included in the wedding, I include several images showing how we photograph children at weddings. If she has let me know she enjoys romantic images, I include examples of that. I also include examples that show her my natural style of photographing weddings.

☐ Personality

One of the most important factors in becoming a successful wedding photographer is personality. A bride needs to have a good feeling about what you will be like at her wedding and how you will treat her and her guests on this special day. These are difficult things to show (and if you say you're great to work with, it often comes off like bragging). So how do you let her know she'll enjoy working with you more than another photographer? I let my past clients tell her. I have assembled an album that includes the nice cards and letters clients have written to me. On one page is the card or letter, and on the other is a photograph from the wedding. I leave this album (or "brag book") out for them to see and read. Happy past clients are my best sales force.

"These littlest participants can add to the overall personality of the wedding album."

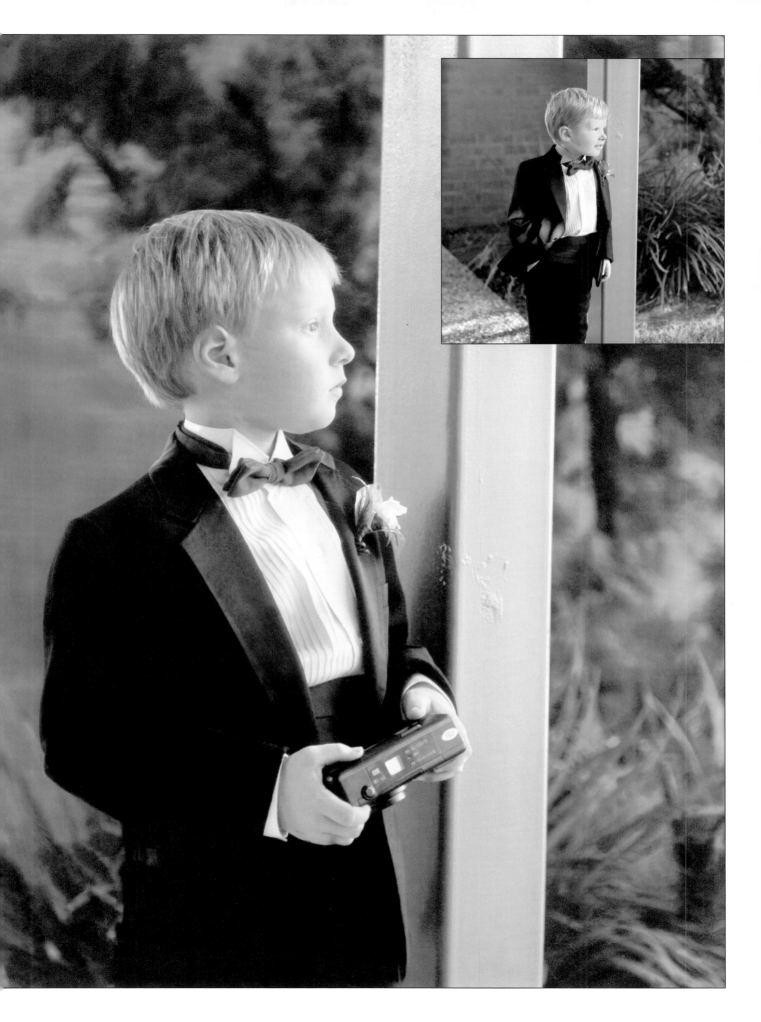

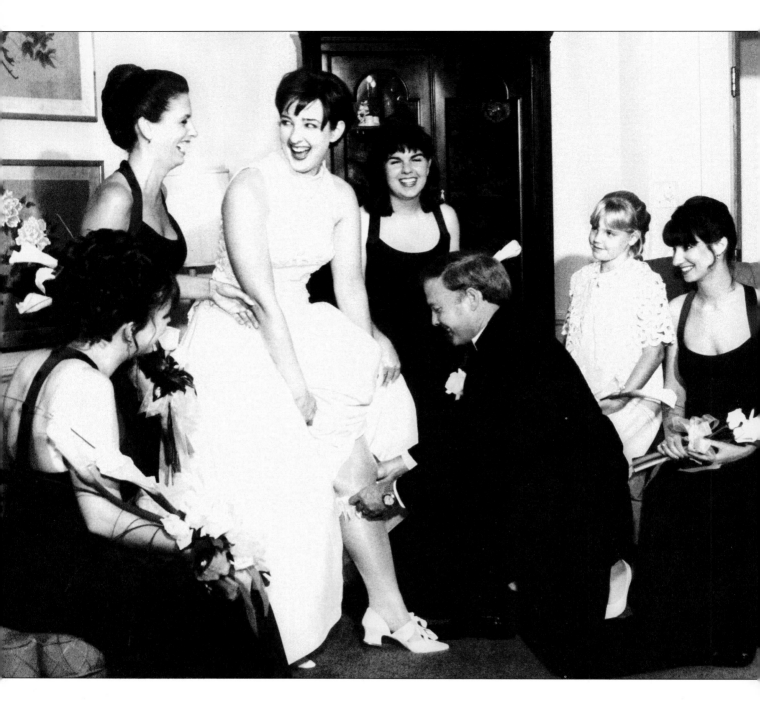

☐ Our Philosophy

We create art-like portraits and wedding albums that tell the personal story of the wedding. The images have a scenic quality, are emotionally charged and have a natural look. We document the day with a combination of traditional, photojournalistic and spontaneous images.

Our experience and professionalism insure the bride and groom won't be dragged away from their guests every few minutes. It's their day; they want to feel special. We help them do that!

Doug and Barbara Box

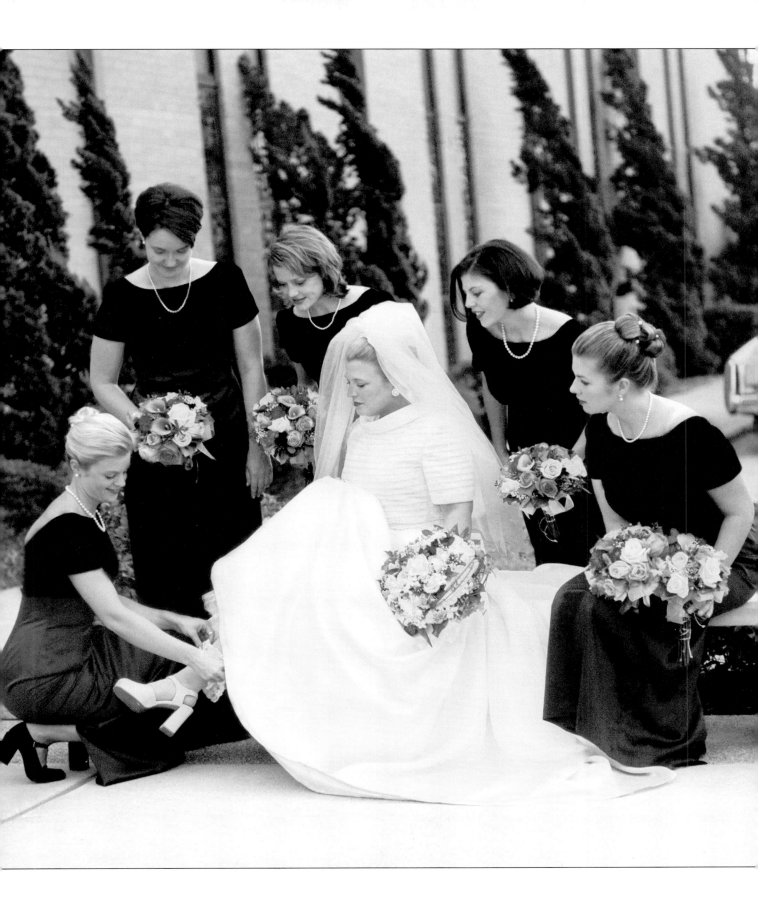

These are just a sample of some of the images I do at weddings. These images are certainly not all of the subjects or groupings that I shoot, and I may not do all of these images at every wedding. Be creative, and look for the unique things happening at each wedding. This list is provided as a tickler list. When you get stuck and can't think of photographs to take, go over this list and see if any of these images fit what is happening at your wedding.

☐ Before the Wedding
The church (outside)
Groom alone (close-up and full length)
Groom and groomsmen
Groom with his immediate family
Groom with brothers and sisters
Groom with parents
Father and mother together
Groom with grandparents
Grandparents alone

Bride alone (close-up and full length)
Bride's bouquet/bridesmaids' flowers
Bride with bridesmaids
Putting on garter, penny in shoe, etc.
Bride with each bridesmaid
Bride with her immediate family
Bride with brothers and sisters
Bride with parents
Father and mother together
Bride with grandparents
Grandparents alone

☐ The Wedding
Mothers being seated
Bride with father walking down aisle
Wedding ceremony (natural light, no flash)
Bride and groom coming down aisle
Hugging shots after wedding
Throwing rice
Leaving church (limousine, carriage, etc.)

☐ Reception
Reception flowers and details around reception hall
Wedding cakes
Toast as it happens
Bride and groom first dance
Bride and groom with parents dance
Everyone dancing
Bride and groom with toasting glasses
Bride and groom toasting
Bride and groom cutting cake
Bride and groom feeding cake
Bride throwing bouquet
Groom taking off garter
Groom throwing garter
Bride and groom with catchers
Hand shot with rings

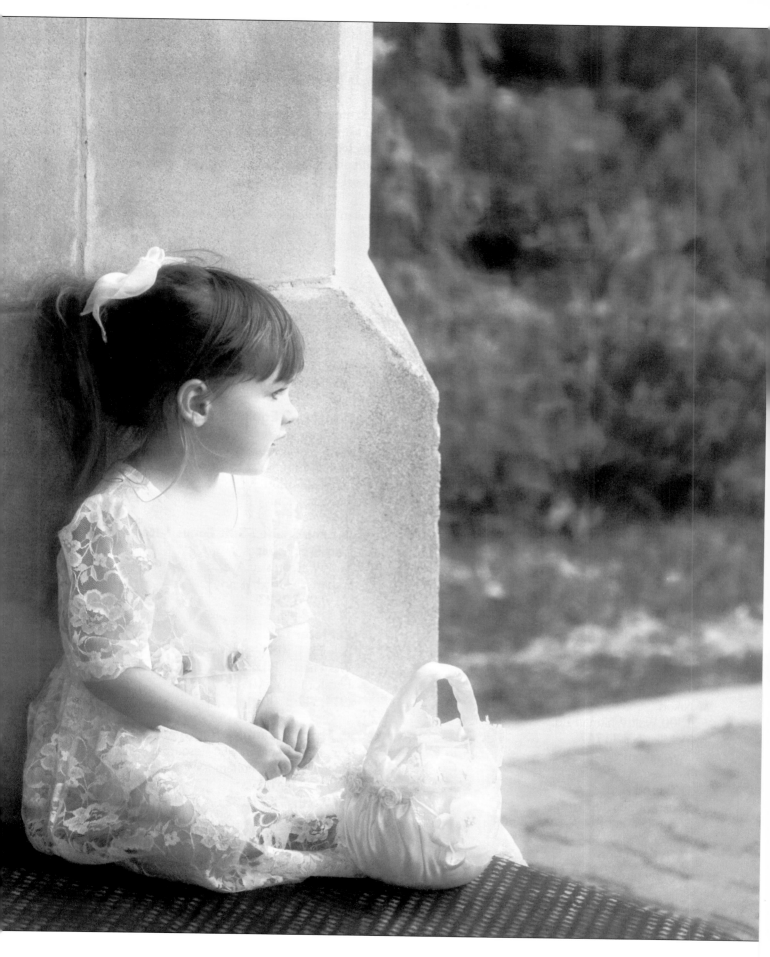

AVAILABLE LIGHT 121

ADDITIONAL INFORMATION AND SUPPLIERS

I want to thank all the people at Ramsey Resources for printing the images in this book. They are not only a great

INDEX

Other Books from
Amherst Media, Inc.

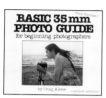

Basic 35mm Photo Guide
Craig Alesse

Great for beginning photographers! Designed to teach 35mm basics step-by-step — completely illustrated. Features the latest cameras. Includes: 35mm automatic, semi-automatic cameras, camera handling, *f*-stops, shutter speeds, and more! $12.95 list, 9x8, 112p, 178 photos, order no. 1051.

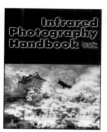

Infrared Photography Handbook
Laurie White

Covers b&w infrared photography: focus, lenses, film loading, film speed rating, heat sensitivity, batch testing, paper stocks, and filters. Photos illustrate IR film in portrait, landscape, and architectural photography. $29.95 list, 8½x11, 104p, 50 b&w photos, charts & diagrams, order no. 1419.

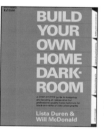

Build Your Own Home Darkroom
Lista Duren & Will McDonald

This classic book teaches you how to build a high quality, inexpensive darkroom in your basement, spare room, or almost anywhere. Includes valuable information on: darkroom design, woodworking, tools, and more! $17.95 list, 8½x11, 160p, order no. 1092.

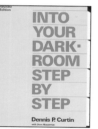

Into Your Darkroom Step-by-Step
Dennis P. Curtin

This is the ideal beginning darkroom guide. Easy to follow and fully illustrated each step of the way. Includes information on: the equipment you'll need, set-up, making proof sheets and much more! $17.95 list, 8½x11, 90p, hundreds of photos, order no. 1093.

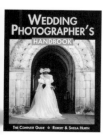

Wedding Photographer's Handbook
Robert and Sheila Hurth

A complete step-by-step guide to succeeding in the world of wedding photography. Packed with shooting tips, equipment lists, must-get photo lists, business strategies, and much more! $24.95 list, 8½x11, 176p, index, b&w and color photos, diagrams, order no. 1485.

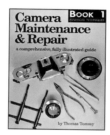

Lighting for People Photography
Stephen Crain

The complete guide to lighting. Includes: set-ups, equipment information, strobe and natural lighting, and much more! Features diagrams, illustrations, and exercises for practicing the techniques discussed in each chapter. $29.95 list, 8½x11, 112p, b&w and color photos, glossary, index, order no. 1296.

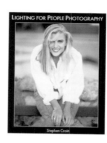

Camera Maintenance & Repair Book 1
Thomas Tomosy

A step-by-step, illustrated guide by a master camera repair technician. Includes: testing camera functions, general maintenance, basic tools needed and where to get them, basic repairs for accessories, camera electronics, plus "quick tips" for maintenance and more! $29.95 list, 8½x11, 176p, order no. 1158.

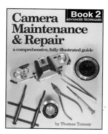

Camera Maintenance & Repair Book 2
Thomas Tomosy

Build on the basics covered Book 1, with advanced techniques. Includes: mechanical and electronic SLRs, zoom lenses, medium format cameras, and more. Features models not included in the Book 1. $29.95 list, 8½x11, 176p, 150+ photos, charts, tables, appendices, index, glossary, order no. 1558.

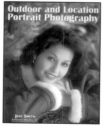

Outdoor and Location Portrait Photography
Jeff Smith

Learn how to work with natural light, select locations, and make clients look their best. Step-by-step discussions and helpful illustrations teach you the techniques you need to shoot outdoor portraits like a pro! $29.95 list, 8½x11, 128p, b&w and color photos, index, order no. 1632.

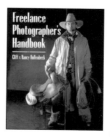

Freelance Photographer's Handbook
Cliff & Nancy Hollenbeck

Whether you want to be a freelance photographer or are looking for tips to improve your current freelance business, this volume is packed with ideas for creating and maintaining a successful freelance business. $29.95 list, 8½x11, 107p, 100 b&w and color photos, index, glossary, order no. 1633.

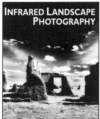

Infrared Landscape Photography

Todd Damiano

Landscapes shot with infrared can become breathtaking and ghostly images. The author analyzes over fifty of his most compelling photographs to teach you the techniques you need to capture landscapes with infrared. $29.95 list, 8½x11, 120p, b&w photos, index, order no. 1636.

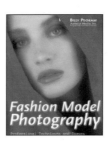

Fashion Model Photography

Billy Pegram

For the photographer interested in shooting commercial model assignments, or working with models to create portfolios. Includes techniques for dramatic composition, posing, selection of clothing and more! $29.95 list, 8½x11, 120p, 58 photos, index, order no. 1640.

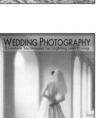

Wedding Photography:
Creative Techniques for Lighting and Posing

Rick Ferro

Creative techniques for lighting and posing wedding portraits that will set your work apart from the competition. Covers every phase of wedding photography. $29.95 list, 8½x11, 128p, b&w and color photos, index, order no. 1649.

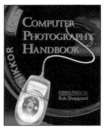

Computer Photography Handbook

Rob Sheppard

Learn to make the most of your photographs using computer technology! From creating images with digital cameras, to scanning prints and negatives, to manipulating images, you'll learn all the basics of digital imaging. $29.95 list, 8½x11, 128p, 150+ photos, index, order no. 1560.

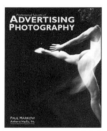

Professional Secrets of Advertising Photography

Paul Markow

No-nonsense information for those interested in the business of advertising photography. Includes: how to catch the attention of art directors, make the best bid, and produce the high-quality images your clients demand. $29.95 list, 8½x11, 128p, 80 photos, index, order no. 1638.

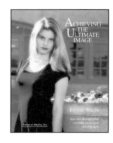

Achieving the Ultimate Image

Ernst Wildi

Ernst Wildi teaches the techniques required to take world class, technically flawless photos. Features exposure, metering, the Zone System, composition, evaluating an image, and more! $29.95 list, 8½x11, 128p, 120 b&w and color photos, index, order no. 1628.

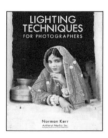

Lighting Techniques for Photographers

Norman Kerr

This book teaches you to predict the effects of light in the final image. It covers the interplay of light qualities, as well as color compensation and manipulation of light and shadow. $29.95 list, 8½x11, 120p, 150+ color and b&w photos, index, order no. 1564.

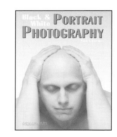

Black & White Portrait Photography

Helen Boursier

Make money with b&w portrait photography. Learn from top b&w shooters! Studio and location techniques, with tips on preparing your subjects, selecting settings and wardrobe, lab techniques, and more! $29.95 list, 8½x11, 128p, 130+ photos, index, order no. 1626

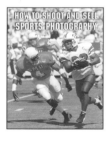

How to Shoot and Sell Sports Photography

David Arndt

A step-by-step guide for amateur photographers, photojournalism students and journalists seeking to develop the skills and knowledge necessary for success in the demanding field of sports photography. $29.95 list, 8½x11, 120p, 111 photos, index, order no. 1631.

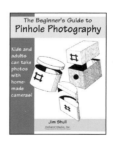

The Beginner's Guide to Pinhole Photography

Jim Shull

Take pictures with a camera you make from stuff you have around the house. Develop and print the results at home! Pinhole photography is fun, inexpensive, educational and challenging. $17.95 list, 8½x11, 80p, 55 photos, charts & diagrams, order no. 1578.

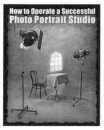

How to Operate a Successful Photo Portrait Studio

John Giolas

Combines photographic techniques with practical business information to create a complete guide book for anyone interested in developing a portrait photography business (or improving an existing business). $29.95 list, 8½x11, 120p, 120 photos, index, order no. 1579.

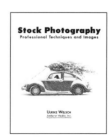

Stock Photography

Ulrike Welsh

This book provides an inside look at the business of stock photography. Explore photographic techniques and business methods that will lead to success shooting stock photos — creating both excellent images and business opportunities. $29.95 list, 8½x11, 120p, 58 photos, index, order no. 1634.

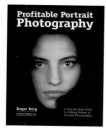

Profitable Portrait Photography

Roger Berg

A step-by-step guide to making money in portrait photography. Combines information on portrait photography with detailed business plans to form a comprehensive manual for starting or improving your business. $29.95 list, 8½x11, 104p, 100 photos, index, order no. 1570

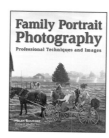

Family Portrait Photography

Helen Boursier

Learn from professionals how to operate a successful portrait studio. Includes: marketing family portraits, advertising, working with clients, posing, lighting, and selection of equipment. Includes images from a variety of top portrait shooters. $29.95 list, 8½x11, 120p, 123 photos, index, order no. 1629.

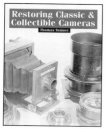

Professional Secrets for Photographing Children

Douglas Allen Box

Covers every aspect of photographing children on location and in the studio. Prepare children and parents for the shoot, select the right clothes capture a child's personality, and shoot story book themes. $29.95 list, 8½x11, 128p, 74 photos, index, order no. 1635.

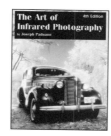

The Art of Infrared Photography, *4th Edition*

Joe Paduano

A practical guide to the art of infrared photography. Tells what to expect and how to control results. Includes: anticipating effects, color infrared, digital infrared, using filters, focusing, developing, printing, handcoloring, toning, and more! $29.95 list, 8½x11, 112p, order no. 1052

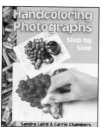

Restoring Classic & Collectible Cameras (Pre-1945)

Thomas Tomosy

Step-by-step instructions show how to restore a classic or vintage camera. Repair mechanical and cosmetic elements to restore your valuable collectibles. $34.95 list, 8½x11, 128p, b&w photos and illus., glossary, index, order no. 1613.

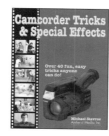

Camcorder Tricks and Special Effects, *revised*

Michael Stavros

Kids and adults can create home videos and mini-masterpieces that audiences will love! Use materials from around the house to simulate an inferno, make subjects transform, create exotic locations, and more. Works with any camcorder. $17.95 list, 8½x11, 80p, order no. 1482.

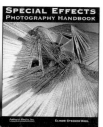

Handcoloring Photographs Step-by-Step

Sandra Laird & Carey Chambers

Learn to handcolor photographs step-by-step with the new standard in handcoloring reference books. Covers a variety of coloring media and techniques with plenty of colorful photographic examples. $29.95 list, 8½x11, 112p, 100+ color and b&w photos, order no. 1543.

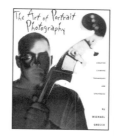

The Art of Portrait Photography

Michael Grecco

Michael Grecco reveals the secrets behind his dramatic portraits which have appeared in magazines such as *Rolling Stone* and *Entertainment Weekly*. Includes: lighting, posing, creative development, and more! $29.95 list, 8½x11, 128p, order no. 1651.

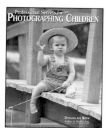

Special Effects Photography Handbook

Elinor Stecker-Orel

Create magic on film with special effects! Little or no additional equipment required, use things you probably have around the house. Step-by-step instructions guide you through each effect. $29.95 list, 8½x11, 112p, 80+ color and b&w photos, index, glossary, order no. 1614.

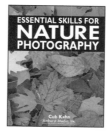

Essential Skills for Nature Photography

Cub Kahn

Learn all the skills you need to capture landscapes, animals, flowers and the entire natural world on film. Includes: selecting equipment, choosing locations, evaluating compositions, filters, and much more! $29.95 list, 8½x11, 128p, order no. 1652.

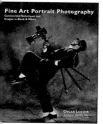

Fine Art Portrait Photography

Oscar Lozoya

The author examines a selection of his best photographs, and provides detailed technical information about how he created each. Lighting diagrams accompany each photograph. $29.95 list, 8½x11, 128p, 58 photos, index, order no. 1630.

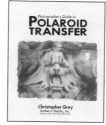

Photographer's Guide to Polaroid Transfer

Christopher Grey

Step-by-step instructions make it easy to master Polaroid transfer and emulsion lift-off techniques and add new dimensions to your photographic imaging. Fully illustrated every step of the way to ensure good results the very first time! $29.95 list, 8½x11, 128p, order no. 1653.

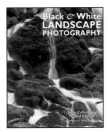

Black & White Landscape Photography

John Collett and David Collett

Master the art of b&w landscape photography. Includes: selecting equipment (cameras, lenses, filters, etc.) for landscape photography, shooting in the field, using the Zone System, and printing your images for professional results. $29.95 list, 8½x11, 128p, order no. 1654.

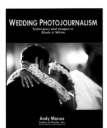

Wedding Photojournalism

Andy Marcus

Learn the art of creating dramatic unposed wedding portraits. Working through the wedding from start to finish you'll learn where to be, what to look for and how to capture it on film. A hot technique for contemporary wedding albums! $29.95 list, 8½x11, 128p, order no. 1656.

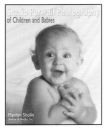

Studio Portrait Photography of Children and Babies

Marilyn Sholin

Learn to work with the youngest portrait clients to create images that will be treasured for years to come. Includes tips for working with kids at every developmental stage, from infant to pre-schooler. Features: lighting, posing and much more! $29.95 list, 8½x11, 128p, order no. 1657.

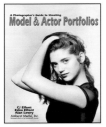

Photographer's Guide to Shooting Model & Actor Portfolios

CJ Elfont, Edna Elfont and Alan Lowry

Learn to create outstanding images for actors and models, whether they are looking for work in fashion, theater, television, or the big screen. Included is all the business, photographic and professional information you need to succeed! $29.95 list, 8½x11, 128p, order no. 1659.

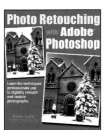

Photo Retouching with Adobe Photoshop

Gwen Lute

Designed for photographers, this manual teaches every phase of the process, from scanning to final output. Learn to restore damaged photos, correct imperfections, create realistic composite images and correct for dazzling color. $29.95 list, 8½x11, 128p, order no. 1660.

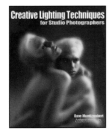

Creative Lighting Techniques for Studio Photographers

Dave Montizambert

Master studio lighting and gain complete creative control over your images. Whether you are shooting portraits, cars, table-top or any other subject, Dave Montizambert teaches you the skills you need to confidently create with light. $29.95 list, 8½x11, 128p, order no. 1666.

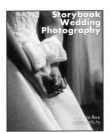

Storybook Wedding Photography

Barbara Box

Barbara and her husband shoot as a team at weddings. Here, she shows you how to create outstanding candids (which are her specialty), and combine them with formal portraits (her husband's specialty) to create a unique wedding album. $29.95 list, 8½x11, 128p, order no. 1667.

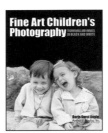

Fine Art Children's Photography

Doris Carol Doyle

Learn to create fine art portraits of children in black & white. Included is information on: posing, lighting for studio portraits, shooting on location, clothing selection, working with kids and parents, and much more! $29.95 list, 8½x11, 128p, order no. 1668.

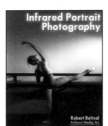

Infrared Portrait Photography

Richard Beitzel

Discover the unique beauty of infrared portraits, and learn to create them yourself. Included is information on: shooting with infrared, selecting subjects and settings, filtration, lighting, and much more! $29.95 list, 8½x11, 128p, order no. 1669.

Amherst Media's Customer Registration Form

Please fill out this sheet and send or fax to receive free information about future publications from Amherst Media.

Customer Information

Date

Name

Street or Box #

City   State

Zip Code

Phone ( )   Fax ( )

Optional Information

I bought *Professional Secrets of Wedding Photography* because

I found these chapters to be most useful

I purchased the book from

City   State

I would like to see more books about

I purchase [   ] books per year

Additional comments

FAX to: 1-800-622-3298

①

②

Name_____
Address_____
City_____State_____
Zip_____ — _____

Amherst Media, Inc.
PO Box 586
Buffalo, NY 14226

③